LIVING
ABOARD

GORDON & JANET GROENE

Editor: Ellen Harden

Bristol Fashion Publications, Inc.
Harrisburg, Pennsylvania

Living Aboard -- *Gordon & Janet Groene*

Published by Bristol Fashion Publications, Inc.

ISBN: 1-892216-27-2
LCCN: 00-133158

Contribution acknowledgments

Cover Photos: Summerset Houseboats, Hatteras Yachts, C&C Yachts
Inside Graphics/Photos: As noted
Cover Design: John P. Kaufman

REVIEWS

Good Old Boat
Rachel Apter & Dion Kolliopoulos

Living Aboard is a wonderful guide for all who ponder turning a boat into their home, for those who have already made up their minds and are preparing to pack up and do it, and for those who are living aboard.

Southern Boating
Jerry Renninger

In the course of 20 chapters the Groenes touch on everything from what the prudent liveaboard looks for in terms of storage to proper illumination for the saloon.

Knowledge of boats is one thing; knowing how to live aboard is another. If you are considering the latter, buy this book.

Preface

So you want to live aboard a boat? Come on in, the water's fine! It isn't the purpose of this book to tell you whether you need a ketch or yawl, how to anchor, or how to take a sun sight with a sextant. A sailboat was our home for ten years, but your dream might be to move aboard a houseboat, trawler, speedboat, megayacht, or even a trailerable houseboat that also doubles as an RV.

We chose to head for Florida, the Keys, and the Bahamas. You, however, might prefer to cruise a mountain lake, the canals and rivers of Europe, the islands of the Caribbean, the California Delta, or the Tennessee Valley, or sail all the way around the world.

Our choice was to cruise constantly, in passages no more than three or four days at sea, staying in anchorages or marinas no more than a month. Still, we are all different. You may want to sail around the world nonstop, or to live on board at one marina for years, going to jobs on shore each day. Some liveaboards never leave their berth for months and even years.

Some liveaboards are retirees. Others are young parents, who want to take their children on a world cruise lasting several years. Still others are single, having a last fling before settling down to shore jobs. You may have enough money to live on; others have to work along the way. When we went cruising, we left behind Gordon's dream job as a professional pilot and thought of his Airline Transport Rating only as something to fall back on if we had to refill the savings account. We had enough savings to last a few years if we were careful. Then, as we began selling our books and magazine articles, we began to realize we could continue to cruise forever, without going back to what we now call "real life." With modern electronics, liveaboards of any age can live anywhere in the world and make a living through the Internet.

We started out when Janet was 31 and Gordon was 38. You may be far younger, wanting to live the carefree, liveaboard life before starting a family. Or, you may be an empty-nester, a family with school-age children, or youthful grandparents who love having the grandkids join you for a week here and there. We are a husband-wife team. You could be college chums, a loner, a family of two or three generations, or just partners who complement each others' strengths.

Living aboard, as this book will point out, is not one way of life but a different *modus vivendi* for every person who chooses to make a hull a home. What we all have in common are a love for boats and the water, too little space, too much mildew, and never enough time and money to take advantage of all the wonderful things available to us in every port.

Here's Our Story

Gordon's career path as a professional pilot took us from Ohio, our home state, to down state Illinois. I'd been writing for money since junior high, and was able to find writing jobs in most places Gordon's job took us, but my own career plans hadn't jelled further. Because Gordon's hours were so irregular, I decided to try freelance writing as a way of being at home when he was. Working around his hours, I was able to write when he was gone and enjoy days off when he was at home. I treated freelancing as a business, and was soon selling regularly.

When we decided to sell everything we owned and go to sea, we had a modest savings account but no hope that freelancing could support us. Still, I wrote whenever time allowed, not focusing on boating topics. Gordon polished his skills as a photographer, and soon we were selling illustrated cruising and how-to articles to national boating magazines. We cruised the tropics in winter, put the boat in storage during hurricane season, and bought a used car to take north to visit our families. When we returned to the boat, we sold the car and went cruising again.

In time, we bought a small, diesel RV that would be our summer home while the boat was in storage. Our writing horizons now expanded to general travel and RV travel features. At first, our bank account stopped shrinking and, when it began to grow, we started toying with the idea of staying away permanently. We bought land in central Florida and, after ten years of living full-time on the go, we settled there. In the final chapter, we'll cover The Road Back, for those who want to, or have to, move back ashore.

Our assignments now take us all over the world on boats of all sizes, from canoes to "love boat" cruise liners. Our credits include thousands of magazine and newspaper articles and more than a dozen books. We owe it all to making the big break with convention, and taking up life on a boat.

Plus Ça Change...

A lot of water has gone over the hull since the first edition of this book appeared in the 1980s. The most dramatic changes have been in electronics. When a stranded sailor was rescued in a remote ocean after making a Mayday call on a cell phone from inside a capsized hull, we realized how awesome the revolution has been. The electronic revolution extends to everything from entertainment electronics to schooling, communications, and navigation. You may choose to do without them and continue living the carefree, simple life, but most of today's liveaboards wouldn't be out there at all if it weren't for the comforts and security provided by the new techno-cyber e-miracles.

Other major changes have occurred too. It was once

risky to take off with little money, counting on finding jobs along the way. Today thousands of temporary jobs exist almost everywhere -- far more than employers can fill. Any American citizen with willingness to work, clean appearance, and basic skills, can find work to keep cruising the United States forever. Don't expect great pay the money will be enough to get by and not much more.

Of course, things get more complicated when you are outside your home country and must have a visa or work permit. Thanks to the Internet, however, an e-business can be conducted anywhere in the world. Where once home schooling was unknown except to missionaries, diplomats, and families that traveled with the circus, it is now commonplace. Today's parents have a wide range of affordable ways to educate their children while cruising worldwide. Living aboard has never been better.

For everyone who wants to live aboard a boat of any size or type, here's how.

Gordon & Janet Groene

TABLE OF CONTENTS

Chapter One
Getting Started

We rocketed back into the welcome shelter of Port Everglades on a rising tide and a friendly, following wind. It had been an exhilarating, exhausting day of sunburn, rope burn, and bridge burning as we faced our first day aboard our 29-foot sloop *Sans Souci.*

Everything we owned had come south with us in our minivan. The boat, purchased a few months earlier, had been in storage while we went back to Illinois to shed the job, our home, and most of the possessions we had amassed in 13 years of marriage. After buying the boat, we worked feverishly to build and sew things for the boat, then we sold most of Gordon's shop tools as well as all the furniture, lawn mower, antiques we had restored, collectibles that had once been important to us, the ice skates, gifts we had given each other. Everything. Then I cried my eyes out, pulled up my socks, and faced the new life head on.

We had never sailed in our lives except for a one-hour sailboard rental during a business trip to Grand Bahama. Yet Gordon's experience as a pilot had trained him for most of the sailing, pilotage, map reading, navigation, and mechanical savvy that the boat presented. As a child, he had lived on a small lake, where he learned to row, stow, anchor, and "mess about in small boats" after building a pram out of junk left behind at a building site. He was an instinctive seaman, amazing me with his knowledge of how to dock, anchor, tie knots, fine-tune the sails, find the merest speck in a big ocean, and come up with a Plan B when Plan A failed. The one thing he had neglected was learning to swim.

For the first three nights in Fort Lauderdale, we slept in a hotel and worked on the boat by day. We no longer had jobs or income, and had to move aboard the boat as soon as possible. Soon we were living amidst the mess for the two weeks it took to commission the boat. Today had been our first sail and, when I realized that I didn't know how to bring the boat about if Gordon fell overboard, I went to pieces. So, we made a deal. That night, Gordon jumped into the hotel pool and stayed there until he could tread water and, the next day, I learned Man Overboard maneuvers under power and sail.

All at once, we were ready for a shakedown cruise down the Florida Keys. There had been many, thudding culture shocks in our transition from comfortable suburbanites to routeless, rootless liveaboards. One occurred when we couldn't cash a cashier's check in a Fort Lauderdale discount store. In another store where we bought galley equipment, our travelers checks were refused too. Back in Illinois, we had been known and respected. Here, we were nobodies.

Many communities don't like liveaboards, perceiving them as freeloaders who don't pay taxes. Good anchorages everywhere are being closed to overnighters in an effort to keep liveaboards from settling in. With no place else to go now, we motored into a seedy marina and paid a dockage fee that, computed on a monthly basis, was more than the mortgage payments had been on our 10-room house back in Illinois. We slept fitfully, wondering what new defeats we would suffer in our victory over the rat race.

The best way to describe the liveaboard life is probably to list what it is not. It is not a way to escape yourself, a bad marriage, taxes, or responsibility. It is not an island idyll, a free lunch, a free ride, or the way to write the Great American Novel. It won't cure your addiction to cigarettes, drugs, or alcohol. These days, with more people living aboard than ever before, it isn't even an escape from crime, pollution, or crowding. Our nearest marina neighbor was hardly 36 inches away. Living aboard is so commonplace today, it's almost mainstream, so don't expect awe, admiration, or even a mild gee whiz. The only envy ever voiced to us was that of men who wanted to live aboard but couldn't talk their wives into it. From the wives, we got only hostility or quizzing looks that clearly said, "You're out of your minds."

Lastly and most surprisingly, we found that living aboard does not provide freedom. We were free now from winter, jobs, and a house that didn't move, but our new masters were the tides, weather in all its moods, petty bureaucrats, and a constant need to provide everything for ourselves including water, sewage disposal, and electricity -- utilities that homeowners take for granted. Half the time, living aboard is hardly comfortable, let alone chic.

With that out of the way, let's get to the good stuff. Living on your boat can be a low-cost way to go anywhere in the world where waterways exist. It can be more exciting, rewarding, educational, and inspiring than any other way of life. It can be a warm, family-bonding way to raise responsible, smart kids. In the great, global brotherhood of liveaboards, you make lifelong friends. Living aboard is a way to travel without a suitcase, carrying everything you need to wear and work with, and much of what you will eat. You don't just visit a variety of cultures as vacationers do. You live among them for as long as you like.

Living aboard, you can test yourself to your physical, emotional, spiritual, and psychological limits. It is a way to grow, to achieve, to take control of your life.

The first step comes well before buying the boat. It is to make the commitment, an honest agreement with yourself and your partners that this is something you all want to do. A boat can be a shrewd investment, but not if you buy on impulse and sell in a panic after a family showdown. Any raw edges in your relationship(s) will unravel quickly in the close quarters of boat living. Hammer it all out on shore where you'll still have room to throw crockery at each other.

After making the decision, your next steps will be to

research the boat purchase, buy and equip the boat, take on the challenges of boat life step by step, and, lastly, make the transition out of boat life just as graciously, lovingly and economically as you did moving aboard.

In the privacy of your boudoir, you have decided to take up life afloat. Even so, it may not be best to make a public announcement just yet. It took us three years to get our ship together. If we had been yammering about it all that time, we would have bored our landlocked friends beyond all caring. Keeping mum was better socially, and better in the workplace. When we began selling out, we didn't appear to be as desperate as we really were. Besides, keeping quiet for a while gave us the option of backing out without looking like fools.

Recently, we had dinner with a couple who had spent years readying their boat for the Big Cruise. They had backups for their backups. They knew all the answers, even when surrounded by older, wiser, liveaboards and ex-liveaboards. Nobody could tell them anything. When their e-mail began coming back about one disaster after another, from domestic ports and not from the exotic locales they had said they would visit, they were a laughingstock.

Everyone who lives aboard has a different story of how it all began. For many, moving aboard comes at a pivotal time of life such as graduation, marriage, divorce, retirement, or getting the children through some milestone such as potty training, college, or marriage. Others must work out arrangements for the care of elderly parents or a disabled sibling. For a lucky few, living aboard becomes possible due to a windfall such as an inheritance, lottery win, or legal settlement. For others, one straw breaks the camel's back and they leave the job or the spouse and run away to sea.

Most of us, though, simply get the liveaboard bug and begin building towards our goal slowly and steadily, over months and even years. Gordon had spent years to reach his career goal in corporate aviation. Now he had a job he enjoyed, with a company and coworkers that were tops. Both of us liked living in a small city, where he could get to work on a road with only one traffic light, and I could do most of my shopping and errands by bicycle. Our neighbors were our best friends, and the corporate future seemed star-spangled.

Then we got word that a valued friend had died in his early 40s of a heart attack. Another friend died young with cancer. Taxes and inflation kept going up. Crime was creeping closer. Illinois summers were beastly hot and the winters were murder. We began to look more closely at what we really wanted and decided it was to be together all day, every day, to cruise, and to pay the piper tomorrow -- if tomorrow ever came.

"You wouldn't have any choice if you had children," many people have grumbled to us. Yet, living aboard, we met many people who lived aboard *because* of their children, not despite them. Some parents wanted to get their children out of schools that were physically dangerous and academically flawed. Others simply wanted to travel widely and share the adventures with their kids.

In any case, hammer it out ahead of time. We have seen too many marriages come unglued because one partner wanted to stop cruising, get a house with a picket fence, and raise conventional kids in a conventional way. Even with older couples, there is tension when Grandma wants to spend more time with the grandchildren and Grandpa has his heart set on a transatlantic trip. If you really want to move aboard, the children can adapt even easier than you can, so do it. If you really don't want to move aboard, admit it and stop blaming those cute kids of yours.

Will you really be able to hack the liveaboard life? The answer may surprise even you. The sea has a way of cutting one down to size, especially when it becomes your home. Seasickness can be devastating. Although Gordon had blithely weathered a typhoon while crossing the Pacific on a troop ship, he can be miserable for the first few days at sea. And I, a lifelong camper and a practiced boat cook, spent one Thanksgiving in tears because the pumpkin pie I was baking in a seaway slopped out of the pan, despite the gimbals. The pie was ruined and the stove a mess.

We met one couple who had spent three years, working all day every weekend and each day after work, to build their boat. They lasted only a few months because they found out they (1) hated boats, (2) hated boating and (3) hated each other. Another couple labored for years to build their dream boat before the Missus' first sail. On the first day out in sheltered water on a calm day, she went absolutely bonkers with fear. We've known at least three people who actually moved aboard before discovering that they were terrified of boating. Even iron-gutted weekend sailors find that living aboard is another kettle of fish.

The way to sample the cruising life before committing to it is so obvious, we are amazed that we meet so few people who try before they buy. Chartering a boat sounds like a very expensive way to cruise, especially when you are scraping and saving to buy your own boat, but it's cheap compared to the financial and emotional Dunkirk of going through the entire move-aboard scene and then finding you despise the water, the boat, the lifestyle, or all of the above.

When you charter a bareboat, it's likely you will fill every bunk and split the costs. It's often more fun with a crowd, but it is not a true preview of what life will be like when you have everything you own aboard, must do all the boat chores yourself, must think about preserving the boat's capital value for as long as possible, and must operate on a lifelong budget rather than a vacation spending spree.

For a week, most of us can put up with almost anything. Then we go home and fling the laundry into the washer and dryer, take an hour-long soak in the Jacuzzi followed by a long shower, and worry about the restaurant, fuel, and souvenir bills when they come next month. That is why you need to spend at least two, and preferably three or four, weeks aboard the type of boat you want to live on with the person(s) you want to live with.

You'll pay at least $2,000 a week to rent a boat in the 36-40-foot range, but try to work a deal on a longer rental in the off season. If you are not yet a qualified boater, you may not be able to rent a sailboat or power boat, but you don't need prior boating experience to rent a houseboat. Even though your liveaboard vessel may be far different, a houseboat trip will let you sample the constant motion of a boat, fuel costs, small quarters, anchoring, dockage fees, and much more. A yearly guide to houseboat rentals is published by Houseboat magazine, which is found on larger newsstands and at www.houseboating.net. Contact the publication to learn how to purchase the most recent rental guide. Rental power and sail boats are found in national and regional boating magazines.

By the end of two or three weeks aboard a bareboat with only your spouse or partner(s) on board, you will have encountered many things that the one-week charterer doesn't have to worry about: using coin laundries, changing the sheets, cleaning and routine maintenance, provisioning and re-provisioning, filling water and fuel tanks, pumping the holding tank, getting mail, staying in touch with your broker, getting around on shore without a car, nightly anchoring and docking challenges, a few weather scares, rainy days stuck in port with nothing to do, and perhaps some mechanical problems.

Best of all, you'll be living among boat owners as an equal. As a boat shopper, or as a bystander who hangs around the marina, you're an outsider. As a liveaboard, albeit a temporary one, you'll find that other boat owners open up to you about their gripes, their horror stories, the tough lessons they learned, their dreams for the next boat.

The more experience you have aboard boats of all types, the better. You'll have many decisions to make when buying the boat that will be your home: freestanding versus built-in furniture, diesel or gasoline, ketch or sloop, propane versus alcohol stove, conventional or marine refrigeration, what kind of mattress, and much more that we will cover later. During your boat rental, you'll live with one set of circumstances long enough to have definite opinions of what works for you and what features you want to avoid.

Renting a bareboat is a rehearsal that can save months

of work, expense, misunderstandings with your cruising partners, grief, and failure.

Don't break your rice bowl is the Oriental way of saying don't burn your bridges. Take it slowly and with deliberation and due diligence, never losing sight of what is truly important, ashore and afloat, to yourself and your partner (s). Sure, there are people you'd like to give the bird as you flounce off into the sunset. Still, you never know when you might need a job reference from an old boss, a job lead from an old colleague, or a personal reference from a former neighbor.

A gradual, friendly, cooperative transition buys you goodwill for the future. It also allows you time to make the change prudently and economically. It has always been a juggling act to sell one home and buy another without having to make double mortgage payments for a couple of months or sleep in a hotel if you have to vacate one home before the new one is available. It will be far more tricky to quit your job, sell the house and furniture, and move into a boat-- especially a boat that is hundreds of miles away -- and still have a place to sit when the music stops.

At what point should you take irrevocable steps such as quitting your job and selling your home? Perhaps never. If you can get a leave of absence, grab this lifeline. No matter how you hate this job and promise yourself never to return, your current life might look like heaven after your first all-standing jibe or your first night in a wet bed.

Selling the house is another matter, especially in these inflationary, uncertain times. If you sell out now, the same money may not buy you as much as a garden shed in ten years. But, if you rent the house, you could come back to find that the tenants and termites have teamed up to win the real estate demolition derby. If the house could bring in income, and if you plan to come back to your hometown someday, it could make sense to put it in the hands of a rental management company.

In our case, we had no family ties to Danville, and we were sure we could find a kinder climate to call home when and if we decided to settle down. Our decisions was to sell out. We'll never know if we could have made more money by keeping the house. We do know that we no longer had to worry about mortgage payments, pest control, vandalism, changing zoning, management fees, the cost of upkeep and repairs, insurance, taxes, and the ever-present risk of a law suit if someone slipped on the front steps. Besides, the equity in the house represented the bulk of our savings. We needed the money for cruising.

Most liveaboards who rent out their homes have excellent luck, and some have two or more rental properties that bring in a nice income. Still, we have heard many horror stories of liveaboards who had to fly home because tenants skipped town owing months of rent and utilities bills. In another case, the tenants left the house so badly damaged, major structural repairs were needed. All the fixtures, which had been stolen, had to be replaced. In yet another, a local zoning change threatened the character of the neighborhood. The liveaboard flew home for meeting after protest meeting, and ended up losing anyway.

Keeping the furniture is even more of a problem than keeping the house. Furniture rarely appreciates as a house does. Storage space is costly both in monthly rental fees and in deterioration. One of our friends found that all of her heirloom linens had turned to powder while in a storage locker. To keep things from rusting, rotting, and mildewing you'll pay a premium price for a warehouse where temperature and humidity are controlled. "Free" storage can be even worse if Uncle Harry decides to turn his basement into a rec room or if the Petersons, who have your leather sofa in their attic, decide to move to Anchorage.

All the beloved bits and brick-a-brack that clutter our lives ashore are anchors that weigh upon the would-be liveaboard. Choosing the boat and selling the house are easy compared to selling the Mustang you've been restoring, or your Dresden collection, or the baby grand piano complete with marble bust of Mozart.

Leaving our home and possessions was a very difficult time for us, made tougher by the stock characters who are inevitably cast in life's dramas. You've seen families torn apart by arguments over who gets what when someone dies. Many of these same conflicts occur when you break up housekeeping. Vultures gather. We were lucky to have supportive family and friends, but some liveaboards carry scars for years from these fracases.

Besides family and friends, you'll deal with a variety of other wheelers and dealers: antique dealers, skinflint used-furniture dealers, long-lost relatives who want back every gift they ever gave you, auctioneers, the greedy, the seedy, and the best and worst of John Q. Public. Steel yourself for a lot of shoving from all directions, and keep your balance.

The best is yet to come.

Support Systems

Organizations and web sites for liveaboards.

Seven Seas Cruising Association, 1525 South Andrews Avenue, Suite 217, Fort Lauderdale, FL 33316, www.ssca.org. Phone 954-463-2431; fax 954-463-7183. Membership is open to full-time liveaboards who live on sailboats. Other classes of membership are also available. Active members receive a superb newsletter and other benefits.

Waterway Radio and Cruising Club, www.jstorm. com/wrcc/ is for cruising boaters who are also radio hams.

www.houseboat.com
www.houseboating.net
www.alt.sailing.asa
www.rec.boats
www.rec.boats/building
www.rec.boats/cruising

Chapter 2
Choosing Your Boat

We promised that this book would be for everyone who wants to live on a boat, not a book about how to choose a sail rig or what kind of ground tackle you'll need for anchoring off Catalina Island. Choosing a boat is like choosing a spouse. You are committing your life, your safety, your ego, your happiness, and a good chunk of cash.

When the boat will also be your home, the decision is even more of a burden-- socially, financially, and practically. It is a huge step and a costly and time-consuming one at that. It becomes even more cumbersome when you live inland and must travel far and wide to research the maritime marketplace. We lived in lower Illinois, where few people had boats of any kind. We spent every vacation looking, from Michigan and Annapolis to Fort Lauderdale, where we finally found our boat. Your search could take you thousands of miles before you find the right boat in the right condition at the right price.

This chapter is about choosing a boat for its *liveaboard* features. Regardless of whether you're looking for a sailboat, powerboat, trailerable, multihull, trawler, or houseboat, it must meet the basic needs of humans who eat, make love, bathe, use the toilet, sleep, fill out IRS forms, celebrate holidays, entertain guests, and so on.

If your home town isn't a good place to find the boat you fancy, study magazines such as *Yachting, Sail, Houseboat,* and *Motor Boating & Sailing*, and tabloids such as *Soundings* or *Boats and Harbors*. Membership in Boat/US (880 South

Pickett Street, Alexandria, VA 22304, www.boatus.com) is a plus for all boat owners. One of the many, many benefits is a newsletter that carries several pages of ads for used boats. In areas where there is a lot of boating, you might also find free "shopper" tabloids filled with boat ads.

If you're shopping for a new boat, go to the biggest boat show you can find. For a list, write NMMA Boat Shows, 600 Third Avenue, New York, NY 10016. Our favorites are the Miami International Boat Show in mid-February for all boats, and the Middle Tennessee Boat Expo in February for freshwater craft including houseboats. There's also a yearly Houseboat Expo. Dozens of excellent shows are available throughout the United States, plus large shows in Puerto Vallerta, Mexico and Toronto in Canada. Fort Lauderdale has very large shows for both new and used boats.

If you want to shop abroad for a boat that you want to move aboard there and cruise overseas for a few years before bringing it back home, try the boat shows in London, Paris, Frankfurt, The Netherlands, Greece, Norway, Ireland, or Sweden. The more boats you see, the more you learn. Shop in-the-water shows, indoor shows, salt water shows, inland shows, winter and summer, east and west, as many as you can afford to attend.

Look, look, look. Read boating magazines. Get out on the water as much as possible. Talk to boat owners and listen to their gripes and horror stories. In Chapter One, we recommended renting a boat for several weeks to get a full taste of the liveaboard life, including listening to the yarns of other cruising folk. They'll open up when you are one of them. Listening is also one of the best things to do at boat shows. In selling their own boat or accessory, many salespersons badmouth the competition. Listen to it all, good and bad, gospel truth and obvious malarkey, and soon you'll have a good overview of air conditioning systems, stove fuels, engines, and so on.

If you're looking for a boat that is also used in rental fleets, you have hit a research goldmine. Talk to the maintenance chief or fleet owner about what holds up and what fails. A houseboat fleet operator once told us that the plywood floors in every one of his Sponge-bottom Specials rotted out in only two years. A bareboat fleet manager in the Virgin Islands told us that every hatch in his fleet of Bedwetter 41s leaked from day one. What we learned was that maybe we didn't want a Spongebottom or a Bedwetter, but if we *did* want to buy one anyway, we could bargain for a deeply discounted price because we knew about their bad points.

Many of our friends got great bargains because they knew that Paperthin Boats used shoddy lay-up in their 1998-99 hulls or that a particular motorsailer was famous for developing dry rot under the cap rails. Like most sailboat shoppers, we were looking for a diesel auxiliary. We found *Sans Souci* and liked everything about her except her gasoline inboard engine, a brand that we had been told had crankshafts made out of popsicle sticks. Mentioning this as a minus, we made a very low offer and got the boat. The truth was, though, that we loved that gasoline inboard. Gordon had spent hours flying gasoline-powered airplanes, so he knew something about living with volatile fuels. When we checked out the story of the bad crankshafts, most turned out to be instances of operator neglect. We got a good boat and a good bargain, and had ten years of smooth, quiet, reliable performance from a "pariah" engine.

Types of Boats

Even if you have been a committed rag sailor or stinkpotter for life, read on. The boat you like for boating, and the boat that will make the best *home* are often different, as many liveaboards learn too late. For example, if you love sailing but will rarely leave the dock, you would have more comfort if you live on a houseboat but keep a dinghy or boardsailer to satisfy your yen to sail. Or, for serious cruising, you may need a deep-draft sailboat plus a peppy little fizzboat for exploring and fishing the shoals. Or, you might live at the dock in an old, pauper- priced power yacht, and use your savings to charter in a different, faraway port each year.

Here are some considerations:

Sailboats

For

There is more grace and loveliness in a sailboat than in almost any other manmade object, and artists have celebrated this beauty throughout the ages. Wind is free, so your fuel costs can be almost nothing. (One year, we used only 24 gallons.) Sailors are an especially friendly lot, independent, resourceful, and clannish. Once you are one of the clan, you belong to a proud fraternity. The right sailboat can take you around the world for peanuts and, even if the engine dies on you (or you have no engine at all), you can mend and re-mend the sails until you get home. Sailboats come in a huge choice of designs, materials, and size. The motion of a sailboat that is properly set up for existing conditions of wind and sea is an easy, natural delight. In addition to serving as your home, a sailboat can also be entered in races that are your hobby or used to take paying passengers on day sails to supplement your income.

Against

The wind doesn't always blow and, when it does, it is often too much wind or from the wrong direction. Sailing teaches humility. Because sailboats must be sleek and sea-kindly, you get less living space per dollar, per board foot, and per linear foot than in boxier designs. A lot of room is taken up by a dual propulsion system made up of mountains of sails plus an engine and fuel tanks. Sailboats usually have deeper draft than other boats of the same length, so your choice of gunkholing areas is limited. The more time you'll spend at docks, the less practical a sailboat is for you. While sailboats are natural and comfortable under sail, they are less comfortable under power than boats designed to run exclusively under power. While wind is free, sails, fittings, and rigging can be very costly. Finally, we find that most sailors run their engines far, far more than they thought they would.

Motorsailers, Trawlers

For

You may have the best of both worlds in a sea-friendly motorboat that is also designed to sail. Most such designs have inside steering stations, so you'll be out of the weather underway. Socially, you're in a happy no-man's land, loved and accepted by both sailors and power boaters. The choice is enormous, ranging from motorsailers that really sail to trawlers with powerful engines and small, steadying sails. Many long-distance cruising families have trawlers or motorsailers. The good ones are handsome, spacious, and ruggedly seaworthy.

Against

While you have the best of both worlds, you also have the worst of both worlds. Some motorsailers are poor sailers, some are poor powerboats, some are both. Such boats have more windage, making them harder to control in a breeze than some sailboats. And, because you're carrying a lot of engine and tankage plus bulky sails, you lose living area.

Powerboats

For

In a powerboat you have speed, power, a boat for serious fishing, and plenty of extra juice for all the creature comforts that run on electricity. Older powerboats with gasoline engines are often a spectacular bargain for liveaboards who will spend a lot of time at the dock. When the price of fuel soars, they become even a greater deal. Yet they have spacious, even downright luxurious, accommodations.

Figure 2-1 Riviera Marine

This Riviera 48 is a liveaboard dream with a master stateroom with bath en suite, two guest staterooms, and a deck fully fitted for big-game fishing.

Powerboats that are well designed are not only fast, but are economical, seaworthy, and able to make ambitious passages. The new diesel yachts are miserly on fuel. You get a lot of living space for the overall length and dollar, excellent resale value if you choose the boat wisely and maintain her well, and years of dependable motoring. Another advantage is that it's easier to learn to drive a powerboat than to sail.

Against

Fuel costs can rise out of sight at any time. Your cruising is limited to where you can buy fuel and how much you can afford. Noise, vibration, and exhaust fumes go everywhere with you. Power yachts have a lot of windage and can be tricky to control. You are totally dependent on mechanical means, which can be a challenge to even the most savvy wrench jockey. Too, a flashy power boat may be a more likely target for thieves, hijackers, and corrupt port officials.

Houseboats
For

In a houseboat, you get more livability for the buck than in any other type of boat. Houseboats don't pretend to be yachts, although lately there has been more of a blurring of distinction, and your fellow houseboaters are easygoing folks who don't care if you talk about upstairs, downstairs, and the bathroom. Houseboats are boxy, which means more usable space per foot of length and beam than in any other boat, and almost surely, you'll also have full headroom throughout. Many houseboats are made for freshwater boating, using non-marine materials at a huge cost savings. House and RV building materials are used, at mass-production prices that give you comforts undreamed of in saltwater craft. Not only do you save on the purchase, but on replacements because doors, windows, and most fixtures in some houseboats are all standard, home builder sizes.

Houseboats offer a great choice of hull type, size, power options, and brands. You can get a houseboat with outboard engine(s), stern drive(s), or gasoline or diesel inboards of almost any size. You can even have a very large houseboat with a very small kicker, to use on lakes that have restrictive horsepower limits. Houseboats have a very shallow draft, ranging from tiptoe- deep pontoon boats to deep-vee designs, so they are ideal for lakes, rivers, and impoundments.

Figure 2-2 Gordon Groene

This houseboat is yet another option for a live aboard.

Against

Houseboats are, socially, the country hicks of boating. Even other powerboat owners may turn up their noses at your square, unseaworthy box. Most houseboats have poor directional stability, making them tiring to drive on long trips. They have massive windage, so they are tricky to dock or anchor in high winds. The same household materials that make a houseboat less expensive than a yacht also make it less durable than a yacht, especially in salt water. Unless you buy a houseboat that is built for use in sea water, you'll face severe rust and corrosion problems within weeks after it gets its first whiff of salt spume.

Another debit for houseboats is that, even though they give you more cubic footage of living area than any other design, they often make poor use of this space. Houseboats have been very slow to provide more than one bathroom, even though sail and power boats that are barely more than 30 feet LOA may have two heads. Houseboat layouts are often clumsy, requiring you to go through a bedroom to get into the head. Most models have freestanding, household-style furniture, not custom built-ins that are common on other boats, so you won't have the storage bins and drawers that are usually found under bunks and settees.

Trailerable Boats

For

Until recent years, liveaboards-to-be might not have considered buying a trailerable boat because most were too small to live on board. Today, however, a large choice of sailboats, powerboats and houseboats can be towed, thanks to an excellent choice of tow vehicles and good trailers. With a trailerable, you have access to every fresh and salt water destination, even landlocked lakes. Instead of making long passages to, say, Florida from California, do it by interstate at 55 miles per hour. We met one couple who cruised the Bahamas every winter and Georgian Bay or the Apostle Islands in Lake Superior each summer. Instead of slogging up the ICW for weeks in the raw temperatures and raucous winds of early spring and late fall, they made the north-south trips in three or four pleasant days of driving. Although the tow vehicle adds expense, it also serves as your ground transport, sightseeing bus, extra closet and, if it has a modest camper cap, your back-country RV.

Against

There is a size limit to what can be towed on the road, so you may not be able to have as large a boat as you would like. The tow car or truck has to be purchased, stored when you're afloat, maintained, and insured. So does the trailer. Concrete cruising isn't free because you'll pay high fuel bills and turnpike tolls plus the cost of tires and other expendables. If you choose not to have your own towing equipment and use a commercial service, per-mile costs are high. And few people would say that hauling a big tow of any kind is easy or fun on the highway.

Summing Up

When shopping for a weekend boat, it's hot news that the boat can hop up on plane in ten seconds, or comes with a free fish finder, or has enough bunks for an entire Cub Scout troop. However, you'll be spending most of your time aboard this boat sleeping, preparing meals, and otherwise performing the plain tasks of living. You may not run the engine more than once a week, but you'll go to bed every night, make breakfast every morning, and expect the toilet to flush on demand.

Any boat is a compromise, but just remember that your needs as a liveaboard will be different from those of all other boat buyers. The choice of boats today is better, more tempting, and more confusing than ever before. Go into the marketplace with your eyes, your options, and your mind open.

It's Deductible

For tax purposes, a boat can qualify as a first or second home just as much as a house, condo, or recreation vehicle. The IRS defines a home as having basic living accommodations such as sleeping space, toilet, and cooking facilities, and a secured loan as one in which a lending institution holds the boat as collateral for the loan.

Each year you'll get a 1098 form from your bank reporting the amount of interest paid on your "home" loan. Enter it on line 10 of your Form 1040, Schedule A. If you did not receive a form 1098, enter the amount on line 11 and provide the lender's name, address, and tax ID number. For more information see your own tax advisor. If you use the boat in your business, or if it serves as your office or other place of business, boating expenses and depreciation may also be deductible.

Figure 2-3 Riviera Marine

Check the main salon for ample and comfortable sitting.

Figure 2-4 Bell Design Group

Constructed in British Columbia, Mary P. is a 91-foot sportfisher with walk-in freezer, two dishwashers, espresso machine, stone countertops, a Jacuzzi, a dazzling master stateroom, and all the comforts of home.

35

Chapter 3
Narrowing the Choice

Once you have decided what basic type of boat you want to be your floating home, you still have a labyrinth of decisions ahead. Boat buyers are concerned about price, quality, suitability for their needs, safety at sea and ashore, economy of operation, resale value, and countless other factors. However, you'll be *living* on board and your choice has to go far beyond these other factors.

Whether your choice is big boat or small, new or used, houseboat or sail, every liveaboard has certain biological needs to be met day by day. They require the right bed, a workable galley, and a head you can live with week in and week out.

The Bed

We humans spend a third of our lives in bed. While you might make do with a pipe berth, quarter berth or a converted sofa for a week or so, the liveaboard's bed is one of the most important, perhaps *the* most important, accommodation. This bed is for sleeping, romancing, reading, staying in bed with a cold, and probably even for weathering even more serious illnesses now and again. During one bad flu outbreak, we were sick in bed for three, miserable weeks of high fevers, fits of coughing, pain and weakness. We were grateful for a real bed, not a convertible or makeshift.

If you'll be making overnight passages, you also need a

bed that provides the rest and security you need in all sea conditions. For serious cruising folks, that may mean two bunks -- one for an everyday bed and another that is used during passage making.

Figure 3-1 Hatteras

No matter how large or small your boat, it's best to have a bed that stays a bed. If it's a conventional size (twin, double, king, queen), it will be easier to buy bed linens.

We have met many liveaboards who manage with convertibles, but it's really best to have a bed that stays a bed day and night. It's tempting to use the forepeak for storage and sleep in the main saloon, or to sleep in the dinette and put paying guests in the master stateroom, but it is wearying to have to make up a bunk night after night, year in and year out.

If one of you is sick and wants to stay in the sack for a day. Or, if one of you wants a nap after lunch. Or if one of you is a lark and the other an owl, you need beds that are beds and dinettes that are dinettes. The more people aboard, the more important it becomes to have separate sleeping areas. Children need their privacy too, in a safe place that will be their own "room" for nights, naps, playing, and homework. We'll talk more later about boating with children.

You may feel foolish at the showroom or boat show, but take out a tape and measure the length and width of every bunk in the boat. Some are too short for people six feet tall and over. Many beds appear to be a conventional size but are actually narrower and shorter than a standard single, queen, or whatever. In the down-size interior of a boat, the eye can be fooled. The tape cannot. Try sitting up in the bunk to see if there is room for reading, breakfast in bed, and basic amorous adventures. If the bed is a convertible, go through the motions of opening it, measuring, and closing it again. It may require more acrobatics than you think. Consider too where the bedding will be stowed if the convertible has to be stripped completely for its day use.

If the vee berth requires a filler piece, try that too. Some were designed by the Marquis de Sade and some by Bozo the Clown. The cushions that look so crisp and natty with their pleats and buttons and cording may feel, when you're sleeping on them, like a hill of boulders. If they are vinyl, they could be cold and crackly in winter, and hot as the hinges of hell in summer.

Although it's important to get a bed that is long, wide and thick enough, beware of getting one that is too big. The huge, playpen-size mattresses often found in big, aft cabins require custom sheets that cost a fortune, and are very difficult to make up. We once lived for a week aboard an aft cabin boat with a vinyl-covered mattress the size of Rhode Island. Trying to tuck in the sheets was like trying to diaper an elephant. And the first time either of us rolled over, they shot out from under the slippery plastic. The other problem with very large bunks is that you can't wedge yourself in during rough seas.

Over the years, we've had excellent service from synthetic foam mattresses. (Not real foam rubber. It weighs too much, smells rubbery, holds water, and eventually disintegrates.) Visit a good foam outlet or a mattress factory to learn about the various grades and thicknesses of synthetic foams. Some are denser, some softer than others. One type has a memory, to conform to your body better. Open-cell foams hold water and, once leaked upon, are almost impossible to dry. Closed-cell foam can be wiped dry.

We recommended a foam mattress that is 4-5 inches thick. If you get too thick a mattress, it can be difficult to turn weekly and to and haul out on deck for regularly sunning and airing. If you'll constantly be lifting the mattress to get at stowage areas under the bed, light weight is a must. Incidentally, if you are buying only a block of foam for making your own mattress, buy a bit oversize to allow room for compression when it's put into the ticking. If your bed is a standard size, simply buy a standard size, zip-on mattress cover (not just a mattress topper) that encloses the entire piece of foam. It's all you need. Incidentally, if you're ordering a custom mattress, order it made with sturdy handles, two on each side and one each top and bottom ends. On a boat, it's important to turn mattresses often to keep them well-aired, and handles make the job of turning a big, floppy hunk of foam much more manageable. .

A custom mattress can also combine one or more different types of foam. You may, for example, want denser foam for more support under your hips and a softer foam under your shoulders, or "memory" foam on one side, and conventional foam on the other.

Conventional bedding is best for the liveaboard boat. Sleeping bags are practical for weekenders, but they're hot for the tropics, difficult to launder, and not very romantic. Crisp, clean sheets and pillow cases atop a fabric-upholstered mattress, with a mattress pad, are what you have now at home. They'll also be the homiest on board. During cold weather, we also use an electric mattress pad from Patented Products Corporation, Box A, Danville OH 43014. Single, double, and other sizes are available in 12-volt or combination 12/115-volt models, with single or dual controls. The company also makes a 12-volt pet mattress.

The Galley

The bed comes first because everyone has to sleep, but not everyone likes to cook. We once read about a man who circumnavigated on an unwavering diet of stoned wheat crackers, fresh sprouts, and almond butter. It filled his nutritional and esthetic needs, and he simply didn't want to bother with anything more. However, all of us eat and many of us enjoy eating, cooking, and serving others, so let's assume you want an adequate galley. Again, the liveaboard's needs are different from those of the part-time boater.

The family that lives ashore can cook at home, and arrive at the boat with ice chests filled with foods they can boil in the bag, microwave, or pop in the oven. Some liveaboards, of course, don't need much of a galley because they shop for deli and convenience foods on the way home from work. Others, like ourselves, provision for months at a time, can our own meats, have equipment to process and preserve fish and any other free food we can find in our cruising, and cook everything from scratch including our daily bread. We cook day in and day out, including Thanksgiving, birthdays, and on the day the engine is out and everything is torn up for maintenance. The liveaboard's culinary show must go on underway, at the dock, at anchor, and on the hard.

The more out of the way your galley is from the general mayhem of boat operation, the better. The cook, engineer, navigator, pilot, and mechanic (in our case, that is two people; Janet is the cook and Gordon is everything else) need and deserve full-time access to their workshops. It's also good to have a galley that's out of the family traffic pattern. In some boats, nobody can get through the passageway to the head if the refrigerator door is open or walk through the saloon if the table leaves are up. A straight-line galley along one side of the saloon puts the cook in the way of fore-and-after traffic and, if you sail on one tack all day, the galley is either falling on you or away from you. For most boats, the best choice is a ushaped galley, out of the way, where the cook can be safely wedged in underway, with all work surfaces within easy reach.

Workshop is the word to keep in mind in choosing or building a boat-home because the galley has to be just that -- not a cute little kitchen that has been squeezed down to doll house proportions. You need a sink large enough to wash cooking pots, a faucet high enough to fill the teakettle, a stove wide enough to hold your biggest skillet, an oven if you can manage one (although we lived happily without), as much counter space as possible including areas that can be used in heavy weather, and stowage space including lockers that you can get into in rough seas or on both tacks. If you want a refrigerator and freezer, they should be suitable to the boat and its power.

While the galley should be out of the way of traffic and engine room maintenance, it should be in an area of the best ventilation possible. Heat, steam, and cooking odors build up in seconds even in large boats because of low overheads. One good spot for the galley is, for instance, at the bottom of the ladder that leads below from a wheel house. Cooking heat then rises to your boat's "second floor" or directly to the outdoors.

Effective, waterproof vents are essential to good galley ventilation in all winds and weather. Even on fair nights, you may have to close up against mosquitoes and "no-see-ums". The more ventilation, the better, yet you also have to guard against drafts that could blow out the cooking flame. It's hard to beat a traditional Charlie Noble. If the boat doesn't come with a good vent, buy one or more from a good marine supply house and install according to manufacturer directions. Buy or make a stove hood with overboard exhaust. Recirculating types are available, but they don't remove most of the steam and odor or any of the heat. Nor do kitchen-style exhaust hoods hold up in the marine environment. You'll be cooking fish, frying bacon, and boiling cabbage and onions on board. The more cooking fumes you can vent to the outside, the less odor and crud you'll have to live with.

While other galley equipment will be saved for the next

chapter, the table should be considered when choosing the boat. It is the nerve center, work center, social center, and sometimes the navigation center of your home afloat. It's one thing to grab a sandwich in the cockpit in weekend boating, but the table in your liveaboard boat is where you will have Christmas dinner, balance the checkbook, play cards with friends, study charts, or knead a big batch of bread.

If the table is not big enough or versatile enough and can't easily be made suitable, look for another boat. We have met liveaboards who regretted for years that their only dining table was on the bridge deck, a long walk from the galley. Others rued purchasing a boat with two small tables in the galley. There was no place to serve four, let alone a larger group.

Again, don't let the salesperson dismiss the galley with a description and wave of the hand. Open and close the table to see all its sizes and positions. Sit down as though dining, to see if it is the right distance from you for comfortable eating and is not too high or low. Open all drawers and locker doors fully, to see how much room you'll have in a flurry of meal making, and how awkward it is to get into bins under the banquette when the table is up or down.

Is there adequate counter space? Places where more work space could be added? If you'll change the stove from kerosene or alcohol to propane, can you find room for the propane tanks? Where will you stow trash? It's the most neglected feature in galley design, especially now that recycling is required at many marinas and you need not just one trash bin, but several.

The Head

The ideal bathroom has acres of room, heated towel racks, a tub the size of a Buick, and a Jacuzzi. Don't laugh. Whirlpool tubs are today's buzzword in large yachts and houseboats. Still, most of us have to settle for less. Authors

Lynn and Larry Pardey wrote about living with their wooden bucket. The sailboat we lived aboard for ten years had only a marine toilet, curtained off between the saloon and the forepeak, and no standing headroom. For showering, we would jump over the side, rinse down with fresh water in the cockpit after a swim, use marina showers or, at anchor when it was too cold to swim, take helmet baths with stove-heated water.

One of the greatest hardships of living aboard was, for us, using marina showers that were usually Spartan, squalid, too hot, or too cold. We managed because we were in the tropics most of the time. On the plus side, some marinas have showers that are so attractive, liveaboards use them rather than their own. So, your need for an onboard shower varies according to what alternatives you have.

In any case, get a stall shower if possible, rather than a handheld shower that wets down the entire head. It's a nuisance to have to chamois the entire cubicle after each shower. Having a shower on board has its drawbacks. Soap scum and mineral scale are always a cleaning problem. Showering makes steam, which adds to the boat's mildew crop. Showering on board means getting the water, heating and pumping it, then dealing with the gray water.

We made two small, easy additions that we recommend for boats of any size or class. A kitchen sink-type sprayer was added to the head. It turned the head into a bidet, and was also handy for cleaning the toilet. We also added the same type of sprayer in the cockpit, cold water only, to use for after-swim rinses.

Privacy is valued by most of us, so the head's location will be important if you have guests on board. It should be accessible to all, not accessed through one of the sleeping compartments. Two heads are better than one. In fact, the more, the better. If you'll be using the boat for hire, guests these days expect a private head, preferably *en suite* and preferably complete with all three essentials, toilet, sink and shower.

Again, beware of miniaturization. The head may *look* standard size, but don't just eyeball it. Sit on the toilet and close the door. We've seen many boats where this was almost impossible. Stand in the shower to see if there is enough headroom. If you are extra tall or heavy, you simply may not fit. Is there room in the head compartment to peel off a wet swim suit, shower, and dress again? Take off your clothes on a cold night, take a hot shower, and bundle up in a cozy robe before venturing out of the warm, steamy bathroom?

The Deck

Boating is, by nature, an outdoors life. You'll be doing a lot of living, reading, sunning, and entertaining on deck, and you'll probably need deck space too to stow tons of extra equipment. Does the boat offer adequate deck space for guests, deck boxes, perhaps an extra ice chest or two, the dinghy and davits, and any PWCs or sail boards you want to carry with you?

Chapter 4
Equipping Your Boat

Just as no one can tell you how to furnish your cottage, condo, or farmhouse, no one else knows how you can best make *your* hull into *your* home. This book isn't a guide to the equipment you need for boating. It's about accommodations for *living* aboard. For additional information, see our book *Creating Comfort Afloat* (Bristol Fashion Publications).

Most would-be liveaboards spend thousands of hours, miles and dollars to buy equipment, right down to the last socket wrench and lemon zester, that they think might be useful on board. Yet it isn't until you have lived aboard for a while that you will know what works, what fits, what gets in the way, what is worth having, what was a waste of money, and what new items you must add. Our recommendation is to move aboard with only the basics, then add new accessories after you see what you really need.

Some of the things we had in the beginning stayed with us for the entire ten years and were used and appreciated daily. Others took up more space than they were worth and were soon scuttled. Still others broke down in the sea environment, and others were reluctantly abandoned in our periodic, but necessary, purges. Many things, of course, were never used but had to be kept on hand for emergencies. Other oddments, such as the clothes one might need for a job interview or a family funeral were kept because it would be difficult to round them up when and if the need arose. Only you can decide if you can live without an eyelash curler, a Monopoly game, or a blacksmith anvil.

It's a nightmare to break up housekeeping and decide what to take, sell, or store. Most of us end up as confused as the man who ran naked from his burning house, carrying only an umbrella and the works of Shakespeare. Decisions on such small things as clothing and kitchenware begin now, and continue for as long as you live aboard. Here are some suggestions for liveaboard equipment that should be added or fine-tuned as early in your liveaboard life as possible.

Lighting

Boats are built, shown, and bought by day. It isn't until you move aboard and the sun goes down that you realize that most production boatbuilders have no clue to the position and amount of lighting you'll need to read at the table, trim potatoes at the sink, find an elusive lemon in the bottom of the reefer, plot positions on charts under blackout conditions, entertain friends with a candlelight dinner, brew a bromo in the middle of the night at anchor, and so on. Your boat's navigation lighting is decided by law according to the type and size of the boat and the waterways you use, so we won't go into that. In addition, you'll also need a good selection of flashlights, signal lights, rescue lights and a powerful spotlight. We also recommend carrying a supply of chemical light sticks, which provide instant and spark-free lighting in an emergency when all other lights fail.

Because wiring and other behind-the-scenes work is required, it's important to plan your lighting early in the building, refurbishing or furnishing of your boat. Liveaboards need good lights for all the tasks that go into boat life: shaving and applying make-up, writing letters, doing the income tax, preparing meals, entertaining, and reading in bed. The more redundancy, the better. Ideally, you'll have at least some 110V lights for when you are on generator or shore power, plus an extensive 12-volt light system, and perhaps some bulkhead-mounted kerosene lamps and candlesticks.

With two, separate electric systems, you can run all your 12-volt lights off the accessory battery that also is used for everything else except engine start. (The engine should have its own battery and electric system, so you can always start the engine no matter how much you've played the radio or TV.) If you can use the additional heat, add a classic Aladdin kerosene lamp for excellent lighting plus a warm glow. You can find a large selection of styles, sizes and types in good marine catalogs. Some are compact and functional. We also have one that is a decorator accessory with its hand-painted glass shade and a shiny brass body.

RV supply stores are a good source of 12-volt lights in all sizes and styles, but avoid portable, 6-volt lanterns and other battery-operated lights sold for camping, as well as those that use white gas. White gas lights and camp stoves aren't safe alternatives for the liveaboard, and batteries are expensive. Too, RV fixtures may be just brass plate, not solid brass, or could contain metals that rust and corrode.

You can't have too many lights. If you need to conserve power, just don't turn them on. Fluorescent lights give bright light for work areas at the chart table, sink and stove. They come in sizes to fit the tightest spaces and they give a lot of lumens for the amperage, but they have two drawbacks. First, they can interfere with sensitive marine electronics if they aren't installed properly. Second, they are very unflattering to the human complexion. Consider adding both mood lights and task lights in the saloon, dining area, and staterooms. Over the bunks, reading lights should focus a bright beam on a book without disturbing a sleeping partner. Halogen lamps are a good choice where brightness and focus are needed, but install them in a way that they can't create hotshots.

Many production boats have automatic lights that go on when a locker door is opened. If you're handy, you can easily add this convenience, or simply mount flashlights in spots where you occasionally need extra light to find something in a dark corner. Boats have so many of them.

In addition to the lights required by the Coast Guard, we also like two sets of lights on deck. One set is bright for security and for doing a repair after dark; dimmer lighting is needed for entertaining on deck on soft, tropical evenings. Courtesy lights take little power and can easily be snapped on to light entryways, steps, and other places where you need secure footing.

Mount switches over your bunk to work the spreader lights, masthead light and horn. If you sense intruders or other trouble, you can flood the deck with light, and sound the horn, before even getting out of bed. At sunup, you can turn off the masthead light, again without getting out of the sack. Home improvement stores have a good choice of high-tech sensors that allow you to trigger lights and other devices by pressure, noise, motion, light or a timer. They range from the most complex, electronic controls to the simple, mechanical timer that can be set to, say, turn off a deck light 20 minutes after you have locked up for the night. With the help of these controls, you can create a three-act drama for security purposes to give the impression that you are aboard when you are not, or are not on board when you are, or are an entire army when actually it is just one of you aboard.

While task and mood lighting are important, the liveaboard also needs a blackout lighting system for night navigation. Work must go on in the galley and perhaps other areas of the boat, as well as at the navigation table, without blinding the helmsman. In crowded harbors, on narrow waterways, or when you are at sea searching for a reef or traffic, night vision must be zealously guarded. One or two darkroom-type lights in the galley, one in the head, and one at the nav station will let liveaboard routines go on. We also carry several flashlights that have optional red shades for use underway at night.

Water Works

Pressure water is taken for granted on most of today's boats, but a lingering folk belief still remains that pressure water means waste. *People* may waste water, but pumps do not. So you may as well have all the versatility, convenience, and economy of running water.

It is hard to control the flow from a manual pump, which gives you a plop of water with each pulse. However, a properly rigged pressure system can give you a tiny trickle to rinse soapy dishes, a teaspoon of water for a recipe, or a fire hose of a shower when water is plentiful. Once you have a pressure system, you can have as many outlets as you wish including at-source or central hot water heater, a cockpit shower, washer-dryer, deck wash down, a wet bar, an ice maker, sink sprayer, and all the comforts of home.

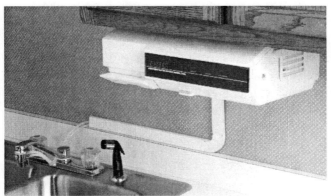

Figure 4-1 Fastek

A water filter is always a plus to assure consistent taste in drinking water. Some mount over or under the counter; others are faucet mounted.

One diaphragm-type pump gave us ten years of quiet, trouble-free service. It drew 4.5 amps while pumping 1.8 gallons per minute at 20 pounds of pressure. If we used 5.4

gallons a day, which was generous for our modest needs aboard a small sailboat, the pump ran a total of only three minutes per day. A reading lamp drawing one amp would use the same amount of current in only 13 minutes. At sea, when conserving both batteries and water, use is far less.

If yours is a power yacht or houseboat, pressure water is taken for granted. However, even the most simple cruising sailboat can have running water if you really want it. One sailor put a five-gallon tank inside the mast. This was filled as needed by a hand pump, then gravity-fed to the head and galley. One advantage to a feeder tank setup is that you keep track of water use in small increments. We saw another boat that had its water tanks under the cockpit seats, again high enough to provide gravity flow to the galley and head.

If you are building or ordering a boat from scratch, stub in water outlets you may want to add later such as an ice maker, wet bar, or soda dispenser. (Yes, some boats have a bar-style dispenser for plain and flavored soda water.) As long as the plumbing is in place, you can add the appliances when you have the time and money. Contact pump manufacturers and outline your needs. They'll explain how to choose a pump based on the number of outlets, maximum suction lift and discharge, and other factors. Then choose a water pump one size larger to allow for additional outlets that will come later.

This is also a good time to add tankage if possible. The more water you have on hand, the longer you can remain independent of marinas. In many parts of the world, drinking water is expensive, of poor quality and sometimes completely non-potable. Aboard a high-tech boat, you'll have your own system to make drinking water out of sea water by using distillation or reverse osmosis. Aboard a low-tech boat, you can devise a way to catch rain water and channel it into your tanks. Even in North America, where municipal water supplies are safe and reliable, some winter liveaboards need large tanks to see them through for weeks at a time because the hose may have to be turned off when temperatures drop below freezing.

No matter where you cruise, drinking water can be a

problem. Every marina's water has a different taste, sometimes high in chlorine or sodium. For consistency in the taste of coffee, tea, reconstituted orange juice and other drinks, it's best to have a good water filter even if you will never cruise third-world nations. We prefer the type that has its own galley faucet, which we use only to draw water for drinking and cooking. Replacement cartridges are expensive, so there is no point in filtering water used for showering and dish washing.

One reason that some boatbuilder-installed pressure systems provide a spasmodic flow is that water goes directly from the pump to the faucet. Water comes in fits and starts, and the pump works on demand. If your system doesn't have a built-in header tank to even out the flow and the pump cycling, add one. It is just a hollow air chamber that maintains a reservoir of pressure. We made ours out of 3-inch diameter PVC pipe. The larger the header tank, the less often the pump has to run.

No matter how elaborate your plumbing system, we recommend adding a stainless steel, quick-disconnect deck fitting that allows your boat to be plugged directly into city water any time you are at a dock. You also need a valve that allows you to turn off this water in case a pipe breaks inside the boat, plus a hose-mounted water pressure reducer to avoid plumbing damage if the city water has a pressure surge, and a check valve to keep your tank water from being pumped overboard if you forget to close the deck valve after disconnecting city water. The deck fitting should also have a good cap to keep out dirt and sea water. Now, instead of having water go to your tank to be pumped to the faucets, your pump rests while the city provides the water pressure.

Hot water systems come in a number of choices. If you have dockside or generator power, the easiest and cheapest choice is a household-type electric tank. Marine sources also sell compact electric heaters in several sizes with optional engine heat exchanger. Through marine suppliers you can also get a bulkhead-mounted gas-fired, at-source water heater. They're common overseas. The drawback is that they serve just one faucet. You'll need one for the head and another for the galley. The advantage is that the water is heated on demand. Energy isn't wasted to keep a large tank of hot water always on hand.

The household plumbing market also offers in-line electric water heaters, which are installed in the plumbing line under each hot water faucet. You need one for each hot water outlet. Again, they work only on demand, so you're heating only as much water as you need. For additional luxury, consider getting a sink-mounted hot water dispenser that supplies near-boiling water for coffee, cocoa, making gelatin, and so on. Ours is a 12-volt model that works off the inverter or off the accessory battery system; 110-volt models are also sold. When we must conserve juice, we turn it off. However, the boat that has plenty of power available at all times can have 200-degree water always on tap.

Galley Stove

The marine stove generates more curses and questions than almost any other appliance aboard. The stove is the heart and core of the galley. Almost every meal depends on it. Many fuels and types of stove are available, and our recommendation is to have at least two ways to cook. Even in our 29-footer, we had the two-burner kerosene Primus stove that was our main cooker plus a one-burner electric hot plate to use when we were on shore power. Such hot plates are far better than carrying many different appliances. One unit serves as coffee maker, waffle iron, corn popper, griddle, slow cooker, egg poacher, tea kettle and electric skillet. Get a top quality, Calrod-type unit with infinite thermostat control, not a cheap, coil-type burner with only Low, Medium, and High settings.

Figure 4-2 Jenn-Air

It's always wise to have more than one way to cook. This Jenn Air range has gas burners plus an electric, down-draft grill.

Figure 4-3 Jenn-Air

Ceramic cooktops double as counter space when cold.

Figure 4-4 InterCon Marketing

Non-pressurized Origo alcohol stoves are now available with oven, door latch, gimbal and other features required by seagoing sailors.

Figure 4-5 Origo

A non-pressurized alcohol stove is a reliable choice for at least one of your cookers.

Figure 4-6 Forespar Products Co.

In addition to your other cookers, it's always wise to have a double-gimbaled stove that can be used under any sea conditions.

You might have, say, an electric stove with a gimballed, bulkhead-mounted alcohol, propane, or kerosene burner as a back-up. Or a propane stove plus a solar oven. Or an iron cookstove that burns coal, wood or kerosene, plus another one- or two-burner stove to use during hot weather when you don't want to stoke up the big stove. Everyone loves microwave ovens, and some boats have no other cooking source. A combination microwave-convection oven makes excellent use of space and energy because it can microwave, bake, broil, or combo-cook (in which a roast cooks quickly with microwaves, yet browns from the convection heat.) Our Dometic combination oven does quadruple duty because it also has a light and a built-in stove hood with overboard exhaust.

Combination alcohol-electric cookers are readily available, and are an ideal choice for the liveaboard who cooks with electricity most of the time anyway. If you have no other back-up, a Sterno stove carries in little space and could mean the difference between hot coffee and a cold breakfast on the day you run out of propane or the marina's power is out. Everyone loves to barbecue, so most liveaboards will also want a portable or stern-mounted charcoal grill.

In the more offbeat category are down-draft stoves, halogen ovens, smooth-surface (ceramic) electric cook tops that double as counter space when cold, and conduction cookers that can be used only with ferrous (iron or stainless steel) cookware. The stove itself does not get hot. Cooking occurs when an electromagnetic field excites molecules in the food itself. I have a one-burner induction cooker (one source is PCD, see the appendix) that is the fastest, hottest heat I've ever seen for wok cooking. Cooks with large galleys may also opt for double ovens or a commercial range, especially if there will be a lot of guests on board. We have seen all the above on boats.

For more about choosing your galley stove(s) and all other equipment, see *Creating Comfort Afloat* (Bristol Fashion). Much will depend on your cruising area and the kinds of fuel available there. If, for example, you spend a lot of time deep in the Bahamas and have to ship propane tanks to Nassau on the mail boat for refilling, you'll need more tankage than the boater who can just hop in the car with the tank and go to the nearest filling station. If you will spend most of your time at anchor and have to start the generator just to heat coffee water in the microwave, electric cooking won't have the appeal it does for the boat owner who has generator or shore power around the clock. If you'll spend all your time in the tropics, microwaving will be cooler and quicker. In the cold, damp Pacific Northwest, there is nothing like a cast iron range that stays warm around the clock, always there to dry towels, warm the cabin, and keep the tea kettle singing. You do, however, have to have a source of coal or wood. Kerosene "pot burner" models are also available.

Unless you specify otherwise when buying a production boat, it's likely to arrive with an alcohol stove. Until now, we have railed against alcohol because it gives less BTUs per dollar and per gallon than almost anything else. On bareboat charters around the world, we have fumed over alcohol's inefficiency, stink and slowness. However, we ate our words after trying a new, Origo, non-pressurized alcohol stove. For our test, we filled it with only one cup of alcohol. It brought two cups of water to a rolling boil in six minutes and 50 minutes later, it was still burning on High. Our propane stove was quicker, but by less than we expected. It brings a pint of water to a boil in four minutes.

Last but not least is the matter of safety, a feature touted by manufacturers of alcohol stoves because an alcohol fire can be doused with water. In our view, all fuels are dangerous. Over the years, we have seen three boats burn to the waterline. Two of the fires started in the galley, one in an electric stove and the other in alcohol. Both were caused by carelessness, not a malfunctioning of the stove. Anything that starts fires is dangerous and any fuel is only as safe as the people and equipment associated with it. Whatever galley stove you select, install it plus its tanks and its plumbing, to the highest marine standards with as many safeguards (sniffers, alarms, automatic shutoff) as technology can provide.

Refrigeration

It's possible to eat well without a refrigerator, freezer or ice, as we have proven in the tropics for months at a time. After a few days of attitude adjustment, we do very well with cool water, freshly-mixed milk, home-canned meat and fish, commercially-canned fruits and vegetables, breads and pastries baked fresh as needed, fresh sprouts that we grow ourselves, and the many fruits and vegetables that keep for days and even weeks without refrigeration (apples, cabbage, onions, potatoes.) However, that is another story. We'll assume that most readers of this book will want lots of refrigerator and freezer space, perhaps more than in a house, and that everyone will want some refrigeration at least some of the time.

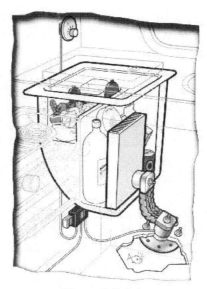

Figure 4-7 Origo

With a kit refrigerator you can turn an existing icebox into a 12-volt refrigerator, or make a refrigerator using a custom cabinet that makes best use of available space.

The biggest and best refrigerator you can get for the money is a household type. With it you can get automatic defrost, an ice maker, ice water dispenser with built-in filter, thermostat control, and other features that may not be available in marine units. If you'll have 24-hour household power available, a kitchen refrigerator is an excellent choice. However, they aren't designed to be turned off for even a few hours a day, and aren't a good choice unless you have full-time power. An exception, however, is a household freezer. If you keep it full, it can keep food frozen on the hottest days with four hours of generator in the morning and four more at night. A custom box with more insulation can do even better.

It's when boaters leave the dock that all sorts of silliness takes over. Cruising sailors shatter the benign quiet of anchorages by running portable generators that would wake the dead. We met one couple who had a tiny, 12-volt icebox that held only a six-pack of beer. It ran off ship's batteries that had to be charged at least four, ear-shattering hours a day. Many others run powerful engines for hours each day for no other purpose than to draw down the holding plates in their refrigerators. We meet countless cruising families whose entire lives revolve around ice and refrigeration.

The biggest drawback to having mechanical refrigeration after you leave the dock is that you can lose it in so many ways. The refrigeration system itself could break down. If the engine or generator or batteries go south, you lose your pot roast because you can't run the compressor or plug in the box or charge the batteries. And, when the boat has to be hauled, as all boats must be at least once a year, you can't use a system that relies on water cooling and an in-water heat sink. Only you can decide how important refrigeration is to you and what price you will pay in dollars, space, noise, mechanical complexity, and exhaust fumes.

Choices

Household units are provided in most houseboats and many power yachts. All you need is fail-safe anchoring so it won't budge in rough seas, and latches that will keep doors closed when the boat rocks and heels. The boat manufacturer will probably give you a choice of models and will provide an electrical outlet and a plumbing line to supply water to the ice maker. If it doesn't have a built-in water filter, add one so you'll be assured of the tastiest, clearest ice.
Be sure too that the drain pan can handle any drippage, no matter how you rock or heel. We've seen decks that disintegrated under household refrigerators that were never meant to go to sea. Drain pans ran over and wood rot went to work almost immediately in boats that were otherwise new and sound.

Custom refrigeration costs much more than any ready-made, but it can provide more cooling area in less space, for less energy, with better insulation, than any other type. You might, for example, start with a conventional, household-type, 110-volt system and provide a super-insulated box, built to fit an odd space, locating the compressor somewhere else in the boat. Unlike a household unit, which discharges its heat into the galley (where it's unwelcome on hot days), a unit with a remote compressor can dump its heat elsewhere into the air or into an underwater heat sink.

You can also custom-make the box to fit available space, using a holding plate that is cooled down once or twice a day by a compressor that runs off the engine, inverter, or generator. With custom refrigeration, you can insulate far better than any commercial unit, reducing the time you have to run the works. You can design a top-opening box that is accessible in any seas, a countertop-level box with a top that serves as work space, or any other configuration that makes optimum use of space. Depending on how you eat and where you cruise, you can use the same mechanism to have a super-size freezer and only minimal refrigerator space, or vice-versa. Or, you may choose to devote the entire box to refrigeration and locate the freezer elsewhere in the boat. With a custom marine system, you can add even more versatility and redundancy.

Combination refrigeration is found on most recreation vehicles, so commercial units are mass-produced at attractive prices. An 11.1 cubic-foot, two-door refrigerator-freezer that operates on 110/12-volt power costs about $3,000. Smaller units are available right down to a minivan size that holds 23 cans of soda and plugs into a cigarette lighter outlet. Also available is a small, three-way unit that operates on 12 volts, household power, and propane. We have a two-way Dometic refrigerator that is more than 30 years old, and it still works perfectly.

Propane refrigeration is rarely seen on boats, partly because of its safety problems (an open flame burns continuously) and also because it must be dead-level to work. However, we knew one cruising sailboat that used it with great success, regardless of what tack was being sailed. If you're *really* into LP gas refrigeration and have a boat big enough to carry a large unit, you can get a full-size propane refrigerator-freezer from Lehman's, the hardware store that supplies non-electric Amish homes. The company also sells kerosene refrigerators.

Note that many combination refrigerators do not have a compressor. Absorption units aren't as quick to recover as compressor units, and they can usually chill down no more than 40 degrees below ambient temperature. On the plus side, they are silent and reliable. On the minus side, they aren't the best choice for the tropics or for torrid, Midwestern summers. We also have a 12-volt icebox that works on the Peltier effect, that is an exchange of temperatures when current is through across two, dissimilar metals. It too is a slow-recovery unit that can cool no more than about 40 degrees below the temperature of the day. However, it makes no sound and it draws little power.

Whatever your choice, we recommend fitting your refrigerator and freezer with an inside probe and outside thermometer that allows you to monitor temperatures without opening the door. The safety of fresh food depends on keeping it below 40 degrees F. (some authorities now say 38 degrees) and frozen foods should be kept at zero. When you are trying to skimp on engine running or battery charging, you risk food poisoning unless you monitor temperatures. The probe can also be hooked to a high-temperature alarm, so you'll have early notice that your ice cream is about to ooze out on the deck in the middle of the night.

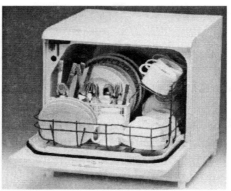

Figure 4-8 Origo

Dishwashers like this Origo SpaceSolver take up very little space and use little water, drawing only 10-15 amps at 115 volts. It can be built in, or used with a faucet connector.

Curtains

To the homeowner, curtains are part of the decor, but to liveaboards they provide needed insulation against heat and cold. They keep the sun from fading upholstery and brightwork. They are the only way to gain privacy at the dock, and they keep thieves from scoping out a quick, bash-and-grab opportunity. Aboard your boat, you need window coverings that close tightly, fabrics that will hold up against bright sun and constant motion, and a style that will be both attractive and practical.

Now on our third or fourth set of homemade curtains, we prefer a medium-weight, white cotton fabric that is thick enough to be opaque for privacy, yet thin enough to provide full brightness below during the day even if the curtains are closed. White doesn't fade in the sun and cotton can be bleached if it mildews or stains. If you want more sun filtering, you can add a reflective lining, window coating, or both. If you are buying decorator fabrics, read labels and avoid any that need to be dry cleaned.

You can make your own, simple curtains inexpensively

and hang them from brass rod or wood dowel. If you're handy, you can also buy one of the commercial curtain "systems" in which channel is mounted permanently over each portlight and a compatible strip is sewn onto each curtain. Once slid into the channel, the curtain can be opened and closed neatly. For most boats, you'll need rods top and bottom to keep the curtain from swaying and chafing underway or to make it hang tight to the portlight at a negative angle.

In any case, avoid store-bought blinds and fixtures unless you are sure they are solid brass or stainless steel. Most household-type hooks and rods will rust very quickly in sea air. One good source of ready-made systems in standard sizes, or equipment for making custom sizes, is the RV marketplace. Just avoid those that have steel parts or replace any steel screws and swivels with stainless.

To go fully first class, bring in a marine decorator who knows how to measure and mount marine draperies. It's one of the trickiest of all the furnishing projects in your boat and, since it is a finishing touch, it's important to get it right. a landlubber decorator, even though professional, may not be equipped to make window coverings for a boat and install them for a lifetime of opening, closing, removing for cleaning, remounting, and the abuse of heat, cold, and harsh sun.

Entertainment Electronics

For many of us, music and television are part of everyday life. Thanks to today's fine selection of household, marine and RV systems that run on 110 or 12 volts, it's possible to have top-quality sight and sound on board at modest cost. If your boat isn't wired for sound, do so as early as possible in the process of adapting her for living aboard. Use the best marine wiring practices and waterproof (not "water resistant" or "splash proof") marine speakers. Sophisticated speakers are available, and you'll be amazed at what great fidelity you get from even a modest system because the boat itself is an ideal sound chamber.

Figure 4-9 Poly-Planar, Inc.

With waterproof marine speakers you can install a good music system on deck and throughout the interior of the boat.

Allow for as much versatility and choice as possible. For example, one central tape deck or CD player could pipe music into the saloon, individual cabins, the head, and the aft deck, individually or all at the same time. When you have guests on board, a nightly musical program played softly throughout the boat for 30-60 minutes after bedtime is a good way to supply privacy for whatever bickering or wooing goes on in each cabin.

If television reception is important to you, the new satellite systems give you access to entertainment and sports worldwide no matter where you are. A marine system with tracking costs $1,500-$8,000 for the equipment plus monthly costs in the $20-$80 range depending on the programming package. Basic equipment serves one television set, or multiple sets tuned to the same program. Costs go up from there.

Many other cruisers are content with a TV antenna plus perhaps, a video recorder or player to supply entertainment when the boat is out of range of broadcast stations. The Internet is replacing the way we receive everything including music, books, TV shows, and movies, so the sky is the limit if your budget allows full-time Internet access via land line or satellite.

As this is being written in early 2000, digital video (DVD) players appear to be outdistancing VCRs but yet another technology may blow them out of the water at any time. VCRs are cheaper, they can record, they are compatible with old TV sets, and they are found in about 93 percent of American homes. At this writing, more than 60,000 movies are available on video tape -- ten times more than are available in DVD, and new movies cost $15 to $35 compared to DVD movies at $20-$30. Rentals are about the same.

DVD resolution is far better than VCRs offer, and so is the sound quality. Models that can record are already coming onto the market, albeit at high prices. DVDs may also be compatible with older television sets, but you may need an adapter. In addition to the superior quality, DVDs can be surfed instantly, so you can start the movie anywhere without rewinding. Another great feature for liveaboards is that they come in portable models with their own screen and speakers. They can be used alone, or plugged into a TV.

The good news is that more VCRs sold in 1999 than ever before, so the technology will be current for a while. So this is a case where you have a genuine choice without fear of having an orphan on your hands before the warranty expires. To take full advantage of DVD, of course, you'll need to design a home theater into your saloon. That means a TV screen of at least 27 inches, surround sound with at least five speakers, plus a powered sub-woofer. If you want to shoot the works, you can easily spend $30,000 on the setup.

For all the sophistication of modern entertainment systems, the liveaboard also needs the homely contribution made by AM-FM radio. In cruising, we gain endless pleasure and insight by listening to local programming. We hear the latest native hits and commercials, learn about local issues and, far out to sea, attend some local church. Once in Nassau, we heard on the radio that a local market was having a sale on dented cans. We raced over, filled our backpacks, and provisioned with enough bargain-priced fruits and vegetables to last for months. Other times, local radio gave us a heads-up on local jail breaks and strikes, allowing us to avoid travel to the wrong parts of town. When you are deep in the islands, local radio stations are also an important way to send and receive messages.

Shore Power Wiring

Boats built for cruising often have little or no provision for using shore power. If you plan to spend time at docks where you're paying for shore power anyway, beef up wiring and add outlets galore to make the most of it. Rechargeable batteries and appliances are a boon to the liveaboard, so provide banks of dedicated plugs for battery chargers and for the Dust Buster, cordless drill, and other appliances.

Even aboard our tiny sailboat, we carried all these 110-volt servants: a heater the size of a cigar box (it heated the entire boat), hair dryer, trouble light, hair clippers, electric razor, blender, hand mixer, saber saw, a couple of fans, soldering iron, and a battery charger. Even though we spent months without shore power, we were well wired to use it to the max. when we could.

Chapter 5
To Quit or To Keep

What do storage warehouses and garage sales have to do with living on a boat? If your present possessions mean anything to you financially, sentimentally, or even socially, sales and storage mean everything.

Some family belongings are beyond price. You don't want to sell them, so you have to store them or give them to another family member who will cherish them as you do. No matter what you do, hard feelings can result. If you give the monogrammed linens to your sister, your sister-in-law will be bummed because it's her kids that bear the family name. If you let Phyllis and Carl keep the silver service, there will be hell to pay if it's stolen or lost in a fire. If Uncle Angus volunteers to make room for the big oak sideboard, you're stuck for a big moving bill when he's transferred to a new job 1,500 miles away.

One couple solved the problem of family bickering by having their goods professionally appraised. They gave all their closest kin an equal amount of Monopoly money and let them "buy" the family pieces they wanted. Those items that weren't "bought" by anyone were then sold with a clear conscience.

After dealing with family heirlooms, you still have to decide what to do with everything else -- some of it nearly worthless, some achingly dear to you, and some of it worth enough to bankroll a good chunk of your cruising year. We chose to sell almost everything except a few antiques, which were left with friends back in Illinois, and some family things that our folks stored in their attic. We gave our friends a signed paper absolving them of liability if our things were burned or stolen, and willing them the items if we died before reclaiming them.

We decided to sell out to the bare walls, allowing almost a full year for the process. We also had to sell the house and give notice at work. Gordon also had a hand in hiring his replacement and easing him into the job. We ran ads for things we used the least: the bicycles, ice skates, guest room furniture, surplus camera equipment. They and the house were all shown by appointment. Meanwhile we worked feverishly on projects for the boat, using shop tools that Gordon would later sell. The heavy-duty sewing machine, we decided, would go with us. The large shop tools were sold, then the living and dining room furniture, and the Porsche, all by appointment. We weren't able to handle hordes of bargain-seekers just yet.

During the last three weeks before we vacated the house, we showed large items by appointment during the week and had massive garage sales on weekends. Luckily, we had a large garage that could be locked up until opening time. Our "sales room" was sheltered from the weather, and the garage was sufficiently enclosed, even with the big front door open, to aid in crowd control. Crowds were crushing, but we were lucky and didn't lose much to shoplifters. We don't, however, recommend letting such mobs into your house.

Here is what we learned during the time we were going through what the British call "selling up".

1. Have the sale in a controllable space and don't let anyone in until the advertised time. People started knocking on our doors the night before.

2. Put up snow fencing or ropes or some other barriers if necessary to keep control of the sales area. Ask trusted friends to help you with the sale and to keep an eye on your house and grounds.

3. Have plenty of bags and boxes on hand.

4. Put a price on everything. Many people are too shy to ask. We used bits of masking tape, which was cheap and

effective.

5. Get plenty of change and devise a way to manage money. A cigar box is fine for a small sale, but we were too swamped to use a cash box. We wore carpenter aprons with money- clipped bills in one pocket, change in another. Have a plan for peeling off bills as the roll grows and securing them in a safe spot.

6. Attend several flea markets and garage sales before you start selling out. Get an idea of what your things are worth. If you aren't a garage sale regular, you'll probably ask too much or too little.

7. Many things are worth more as a tax write-off than you can get for them at a yard sale. We found that expensive books and tailor-made suits wouldn't sell at any price. We donated them and got receipts.

8. If you have a really large household as we did, have several garage sales so everything doesn't have to be put out at once. We had sales three weekends in a row, and some customers came to all three. This gave us a smaller, more manageable inventory each time, with new items each week to entice old and new buyers. Each time someone asked us to come down in price, we stood firm but told them we would be slashing prices on the final afternoon. Most paid our price then and there.

9. Don't overlook Internet sites such as eBay as a way of getting top dollar for your collectibles, antiques, and oddments. The more specialized the item, the less likely you are to get a fair price for it at a yard sale.

10. Have an exit plan for unsold items. A dealer may give you a flat rate or take things away for consignment, or a charity will pick up the leftovers by appointment.

The last things to go were the washer and dryer, followed by our bedroom set and the kitchen appliances. I sat down in the middle of the bare living room carpet and had a good cry. It had been withering to see the treasures of a 13-year marriage appraised, rejected, bargained for, and carried away by strangers. Deciding what to keep and what to sell had been emotionally wearing and we were also physically exhausted. If selling your own household sounds like too much, there are other options.

Auctions

You can avoid the hard work and emotional trauma of selling out by calling in an auctioneer. Then just leave for the afternoon and come back to collect the money. Some liveaboards take this route and never regret it. If you have a large yard, house or barn, have the auction at your place. Otherwise, the auction house trucks things away to their own premises, usually at extra cost. The auctioneer does all the advertising and promotion, gets the best prices possible, and gives you a check for 50-75 percent of the proceeds.

The good thing about an auction is that it is quick and sanitary. You don't even have to be there. A good auctioneer may get more for your goods than you could get yourself. On the minus side, the auctioneer takes a hefty commission, and there is always the chance that your auction will be held on the day of the big rain storm, or the big game, or the day when too many other sales are going on in your area.

Secondhand Dealers

Unless you're utterly desperate, we can't recommend selling everything to a dealer for a lump sum. We called in several and their offers were simply laughable. The upside to this method is that it involves no work, no investment in advertising, and no contact with the public. We had somewhat better luck with consignment houses, which usually take 40-50% of the sale price. If you're in a hurry to leave on your boat, however, consignment sales could take weeks, even months. Another option is to take things to a reputable pawn broker, who will give you 50% of what he or she things the items can bring. Some pawn shops prefer to deal only with people who truly hope to redeem their things when they have the money; others don't care that you're about to leave town and will probably never return.

Storage

Thanks to the explosion in "stuff" just at a time when basements and attics have gone the way of the buggy whip, you have a large choice of places and plans for storing furniture, keepsakes, and anything else that you want to keep but don't want on the boat. One of them will be right for you. We rented a storage cubbyhole in Fort Lauderdale, where we returned yearly for hauling and provisioning. If you plan to be away only for a specified time and will return to the same town someday, find storage there.

On the minus side are the ongoing costs of storage month after month, and of moving it all if you decide later to settle down in San Diego instead of returning to Indiana. Things deteriorate in storage, and there is also the psychological tug of knowing that all the comforts of home are back there waiting for you when you're beating to windward with rain in your face.

Prices vary around the nation but in central Florida, a 10 X 20-foot, private storage room with garage door costs $91-$180 monthly plus state sales tax. For a 10 X 10-foot space you'll pay about $60. Spaces without air conditioning are at the low end of the scale; if you need both heat and air for the controlled environment required to protect furniture and valuables, it will cost far more. Many storage companies put you in touch with an insurance company that specializes in stored items; talk too to your own insurer to see what is available. In any case, insurance is extra and riders for valuables are more still. If you can't move everything to the mini-warehouse yourself, you'll also pay extra for hauling.

Moving companies also offer storage but the cost is prohibitive for most liveaboards. In our area, cost for storing four rooms of furniture is about $250 a month plus insurance and moving. Still, you get first-class service from a company that specializes in handling household goods. Upholstered pieces are put on racks for good air circulation, and the storage facility probably has a sprinkler system and good ventilation. On the minus side, these facilities are not designed to provide you access to your goods. They are stacked in their own area but in one, large room where you are not welcome. It's unlikely you'll see them again until you have them moved out. In a mini-warehouse, by contrast, you arrange your stuff your way. Nobody else touches it, and you can get at it whenever you like.

"It's important to clean everything before putting it away," we were told by storage experts. "If your upholstered furniture and carpets are stained even slightly, the stains will deepen and set in storage. We can't guarantee that things won't rust and mildew."

Before choosing a storage facility, look over the space for its size and shape, the type and security of entire facility and for your individual unit, lighting, and other features. Know whether there's an electric outlet in case you want to run a humidifier or lights. Some warehouses have 24-hour attendants and security including 24-hour access to your stall. Others allow you in only during limited hours.

Banks offer the least convenient access hours, but the best security. Safety deposit boxes are available in many sizes, starting at about $40 a year. In our area, they are offered only by banks. In larger cities, secure and climate-controlled vaults are available for storing valuable paintings and other large items.

The best solution for most of us is a combination of storage methods. When you deal with a professional storage company, you have specified rights and protection (it varies with the company; read the fine print) and you are not inconveniencing friends or relatives. On the other hand, the service is entirely impersonal. Let's say you're cruising somewhere and need a document, or your down-filled vest, or you run short of money and have to sell the flatware. A friend or relative who has your goods in the basement, or who has been signed on for access to your warehouse or safety deposit box, can root around, find what you want, and do what needs to be done. A warehouse attendant cannot.

During our first, three-month, shakedown cruise, we left our van at the boatyard where we had outfitted. Some surplus goods were left in it. Then, fully committed to the liveaboard life, we sold the van and everything was kept on board with us.

Should You Keep the House

Most of us will keep at least some worldly goods, but keeping the house is another matter entirely. If you plan to settle down in your home town again someday, it could make sense to rent the house under professional management and let it grow in value while you're gone. Talk to professionals about their fees. Then do the math about what the house is likely to bring in and what your costs will be for taxes, maintenance, insurance, and predictable repairs (based on the expected life span of shingles, appliances, exterior paint, the garage door opener, and so on.) You'll also need a reserve for unexpected repairs and for uncollected rent when tenants move out and new ones must be found.

Talk to your accountant about the tax consequences of renting rather than selling and paying capital gains. A boat that is your home could constitute a roll-over if you sell the house and replace it with a boat. For tax purposes, a boat also qualifies as a second home. Other factors to consider include homestead exemption, which is lost if the house is no longer owner- occupied.

If you prefer to let it wait for you, complete with furnishings, you can simply slip back into what we call "real life" when your cruising days are done. You'll have to budget for insurance, taxes and maintenance such as yard care. It's essential that a lived-in look be scrupulously maintained, or your insurance company could claim abandonment and refuse to pay if the house is vandalized.

Only you can decide whether it's best financially or otherwise to keep the house. Real estate values could plunge in your area, or skyrocket. After cruising opens your eyes to other locales, you may fall in love with another state, even another country. Or you could find, after your first storm at sea, that you want to go back to the same house in the same town and live happily ever after. As for ourselves, our decision was to sell out almost completely and never look back. In our case, it proved to be the right choice. It's painful to shed an entire way of life, but possessions are a heavy anchor. You may be better off without them.

Chapter 6
Keeping Warm
Keeping Cool

Think for a minute about the amount of space in your house that is devoted to a furnace, fireplace, air conditioning, and all the ducting necessary to keep your home cool enough, warm enough, and free of smoke and fumes. We never thought much about it because we cruise only in the tropics. It wasn't until we spent a week aboard a borrowed 42-footer from the north that we realized how much space it takes to have both central heat and air. The heater itself took up little room, but it seemed that every locker we opened was filled with ducting. The loss of stowage room astonished us.

It's nice to have climate control, but compromises have to be made on a boat. You need the most comfort for the least space and fuel. Think first about simple solutions. It's difficult to increase insulation, as you might in a house by blowing more fiberglass into the attic. So, for boating in areas of extreme heat or cold, consider buying a boat built from materials that insulate well, such as balsa core, rather than thin aluminum or fiberglass. Add insulation where possible. For example, you might replace single portlights with double-glazed, add a layer of batting under ceilings, or blow a layer of foam into voids. Just don't blow two-part foam into places where plumbing or wiring run. It forms a solid glob that would have to be carved away if you needed to get at the pipes or wires.

To insulate the boat's lower living quarters against

cold waters, add thicker carpet and padding or an underlayment under the wood flooring. Adding insulation also reduces noise transference, so you'll have a warmer, cooler, quieter boat. For the full story on insulation via radiant heat barrier, thermal heat barrier, and moisture and air barrier, contact Unlimited Quality Products, 710 Broadway Road #508, Mesa, AZ 85210, 800-528-8219 or www.theinsulator.com. If there is any place on your boat that could be better insulated, they'll have a product that is right for the task.

Second, choose your colors. When we changed our deck color from blue to white, it was 15 degrees cooler down below on a sunny day in the tropics. A northern boat could use darker colors. We were amused to find that a black garbage bag, slipped over a white hatch on a cold, sunny morning, acted like a radiant heater to the saloon below. A treated canvas cockpit enclosure in a trendy hunter green shade could make a difference of 40-50 degrees over a white cover on a sunny day.

Solar film on windows makes a big difference in heat gain. Call in a professional installer for the best choice of films, which range from just a hint of tint to a mirror finish that shuts off up to 80% of the light. A professional can also assure a smooth finish without distortion and peeling. Few do-it-yourselfers can get as good a result.

Heating

Because of its relatively poor insulation, you'll need a larger capacity heater on your boat than for same the cubic footage in a house. You're also concerned about fire safety, safety from CO and other dangerous fumes, and the moisture that all fuels, except electric heat, put into the air. In a house, it's usually difficult to bring humidity up to comfort levels. On a boat, by contrast, clammy cold can add to the discomfort of a winter day.

Figure 6-1 Heater Craft

Operating like a car heater, by circulating the boat's engine cooling water through an air handler, units like this Heater Craft are one way of heating your boat.

Redundancy is our middle name. Just as we recommend having more than one cooking stove, we urge you to have more than one way to heat the boat. You might, for example, have baseboard electric heat to use in port and a heat exchanger-blower arrangement that warms your boat with engine heat underway. Or a built-in diesel furnace plus an electric fireplace that enhances your saloon's decor. Or, in a cold climate such as Scandinavia or the Pacific Northwest, a combination heating-cooking range plus a portable electric heater to warm up cold corners as needed, and a solar heater that kicks in when the sun comes out.

Portable versus Built-in Heaters

Many electric, catalytic, propane, and diesel/kerosene heaters are available in both built- in and portable models. The advantage to portables is that they can be banished to the dock box for the entire summer. In use, they can be placed and aimed anywhere heat is needed, making the least heat provide the most comfort. Portables can easily be taken off the boat for repair or replacement, they are generally inexpensive, and you can take yours with you if you go camping or rent a cabin when vacationing off the boat. And they don't require bulky ducting.

On the minus side, portables spew all their fumes and moisture into the air along with the heat. Even a minor maladjustment can result in a rain of soot or, worse still, a CO hazard. They get in the way, and can be difficult to secure. They can be a serious danger if they tip over or slip out of position when the boat rocks. Electric portables are clean and easy, but all other fuels must be bought, transported, stowed, and refilled regularly.

The advantage to built-ins is that they can be vented outdoors without the massive heat loss suffered when you must open a hatch to use a portable safely. Installed properly, a marine furnace can be used anywhere, any time. It's always there, ready to switch on, in an unexpected cold snap. And there's no worry about it careening around the boat, even in the roughest seas.

Heat from Air Conditioners

Air conditioners are available with heat strips or reverse cycling. The advantage is that one unit does double duty. The heat is dry and without worrisome fumes. Unless you winter south of, say, Charleston, you can't rely on reverse cycling for the amount of heat you'll need in a cold, northern winter. Too, it has the same disadvantages as any other electric heat. It's only as good as the dock power or generator that runs it.

Electric Heating

Electricity produces quick, dry, safe heat. A large selection of electric heaters in many models and sizes is found at discount stores. We have several, one with remote control and another a little giant no larger than a loaf of bread. It's fairly easy to install electric baseboard heat on many boats, especially houseboats.

For those liveaboards who have their own electric meter, or live at marinas that charge extra for electric heat and air, the biggest minus is the high cost of electric heat. Household heaters rust in damp, salt air, so they should get protection and good, preventive care. You'll be without heat if your power source (generator, shore power) fails. Heat is a high-draw item, and not all marinas are wired for high demand on cold days.

Wood, Charcoal, and Coal

Nothing is cozier than a crackling fire in a proper marine stove or fireplace. If you have a good source of inexpensive wood, you can have free heat independent of a generator or shore power. A potbelly stove is also a back-up for cooking if your cookstove fails. Properly installed, it vents smoke and fumes to the outside.

There are many minuses, starting with the ever-present fire danger. Stoves and fireplaces take up space, are dirty, and don't give a lot of BTUs for the bulk or the buck. And, because you need a chimney, you have another hole in the boat. *Charcoal should never be burned in an enclosed space, even under a cockpit awning. As we write this, a woman was found dead in a tent where she was using a charcoal cooker. Burn charcoal only in a properly vented stove or in the open air.*

Propane Furnace

Propane furnaces are used almost universally in recreation vehicles. If you cook with gas, an RV propane furnace may be a logical choice too. Houseboats are especially well suited to this installation. Propane is easily available, fairly inexpensive, hot, clean, and less stinky than some other fuels.

Its drawbacks include the inherent dangers in heaters that involve flames and fumes. Propane isn't commonly sold dockside, so you'll probably have to haul the tanks to refill stations. It must be properly vented to guard against CO_2

poisoning and you'll also need some electricity to run a 110- or 12-volt blower.

Engine Heat Exchange

If you'll be underway a lot, consider using "free" engine heat to warm the cabin. Basically, it requires a heater coil that loops engine cooling water into the cabin, and a blower to distribute the heat. Automotive suppliers sell a ready made, add-on unit that includes a blower, grillwork and housing, and optional thermostatic control.

The disadvantage to using engine heat for your cabin is that you have heat only when the engine is running and for a short time after shutdown. If it's your only heat source, and you have to run the engine just to warm the cabin, it's a very inefficient use of fuel and machinery. Like the heater in your car, this one circulates water that is often at near-boiling. A proper installation, and good maintenance, are mandatory. Any leak could result in bad burns.

Air Conditioning

You have three basic choices for mechanical air conditioning for your boat. A household window unit, an RV rooftop unit, or a marine air conditioning system, portable or built-in.

Household Units

For $100 or less you can get a window unit that will cool an average-size boat. Most brands have a long history of reliability. Repairmen are familiar with them, parts are readily available, and you don't need a house call. Just tote it to the repair shop. No space is lost in the cabin, because the unit hangs out on deck. Off season, remove it and stow it ashore.

On the minus side, these units aren't yachty. In fact,

they're downright lubberly, and ugly to boot. They aren't made for the marine environment, so they'll corrode quickly in salt air. They are noisy, belch all the cold air into one spot, and they dump the waste heat on deck. It would be difficult to make an installation secure enough for use in a seaway, and a heavy unit on a light boat can change the center of gravity and therefore the boat's handling.

Rooftop RV Air Conditioners

It's likely you can find RV units to fit existing hatches, or make an adapter. Many houseboats are factory-equipped with rooftop units to fit standard RV hatches. The flow pattern is more comfortable than most window units we have seen. While they are more expensive than window units, they cost less than marine units. The styling is sleek and streamlined, they are weather resistant, and they can be removed fairly easily for service or off-season storage. We have one rooftop Coleman RV air conditioner that is still reliable after almost 30 years.

One drawback to rooftop units is the noise, which could dislodge barnacles. Hot air is discharged on deck, which is a problem when someone is working or sunbathing there. Like window units, rooftop air conditioners constantly drip condensation, so you have to channel it where it won't start wood rot. The units are heavy and they vibrate, which could be a problem if you mount one where such stresses weren't allowed for by the boat designer. Too, replacing a hatch with a rooftop unit could make your boat much darker down below.

Marine Air Conditioning

The most expensive, efficient and comfortable air conditioning system for your boat- home is a marine system. It is installed below, safe from the elements, and without requiring holes in the deck. Discharge heat goes into the water, not into the air around you. Condensate runs harmlessly into a bilge or sump. Air flow in a good installation is quiet and free of drafts. You can customize the installation to a fare-thee-well, with individual climate control in each cabin if you like and the compressor(s) and condenser(s) in any spot where you have room. Free-standing units are also available, with the same pluses and minuses of other portables.

There are two basic types. In one system, water is chilled and then circulated throughout the boat. In the other, cooled air is blown through ducts. While water chillers have their merits, we find them slow to react to thermostatic changes. They also don't seem to make for as dry a boat as a cooled-air unit. Go to a major boat show and talk to salespersons for both types of AC, and you'll get an earful. Both camps approach air conditioning with almost religious fervor.

The drawbacks of central marine air include the space that must be devoted to the unit, its ducts and air handlers. You'll pay a pretty penny for the initial purchase and installation and, when repairs are needed, a marine specialist must come aboard at premium marine prices.

Whatever air conditioner you choose, note its starting load (not just its running load) to make sure your generator and shore power umbilicals can handle it if the AC, refrigerator and other high-draw items kick in at once.

Breezes

Not all of us can afford the price, space and energy of mechanical air conditioning. You can do a lot with fans, both 110- and 12-volt. We have one that folds flat against a bulkhead when not in use, and a couple of automotive fans at strategic spots. Little fans and blowers use little energy, are available in all sizes, and do yeoman's duty, so go wild with them to boost air conditioner or heater effectiveness. We even have a tiny, 12-volt fan in the reefer to keep cold air circulating more effectively.

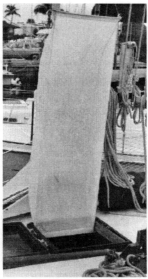

Figure 6-2 Gordon Groene

A simple wind catcher can be sewn from lightweight sail cloth and turned to any direction to catch the breeze.

If you can manage storage space for a big, square, breeze box, either on board or in your dock box, it is a great help for blowing air into or out of the boat when you simply want to air it out or are doing work that requires good ventilation. On sale, a three-speed box costs less than $20. We consider ours an essential part of the maintenance department as well as a comfort convenience.

Vents of all kinds help keep breezes flowing through the boat. Some rely on a large horn that can be turned in any direction to scoop breezes. Others rely on a venturi effect to cram air through the boat. Still others are installed over hot spots (galley stove, shower) to channel warm air away from living quarters. In any boat that goes to sea, the chief concern is that these vents don't become entryways for water. Before you cut a hole in your boat to install a vent, test it. If it leaks now, it will leak later -- into your *home.*

Since most boats move to a variety of docks and anchorages, it's best to have a variety of ventilation aids. When you hang at anchor, your boat usually faces into the wind. At docks, winds could come from any direction. Ready-made wind chutes are inexpensive to buy, but it's best to make your own to fit whatever openings and riggings you will work with. Use lightweight sail material, which can be sewn on a household sewing machine.

It should have (1) a hold-down so it doesn't whip up out of the hatch. (2) It should be long enough to raise high enough on deck to catch the breezes, not blanked by other boats or by equipment on your own deck. (3) It needs some means of holding the "mouth" and "throat" open if the winds die. This can be done with plastic hoops, a wood frame, or by tying off "wings" of the wind chute to the shrouds.

One last suggestion. When you're designing a cockpit enclosure, make it do triple duty as an enclosure, wind scoop, and water catchment. If you can make each wall independent, you can open and close walls as needed to catch the breeze and funnel it below.

Figure 6-3

Figure 6-4 Gordon Groene

One of these hatches opens forward, which means it catches breezes at anchor. The other opens to the rear.

Chapter 7
The Cost of Cruising

As writers who love life on the go, the question we are asked most often is, "How much does it cost to live on a boat?"

Sorry, but at the risk of sounding smart-mouthed, we have to reply, "What does it cost to live in a house? A farm? A three-room apartment?" The answer is that the cost of living depends greatly on *how* you live. Do you play the horses, pay child support, have big dental bills, live on steak instead of beans and rice, hang out at bars? Do you keep your boat Bristol fashion or let things slide? When you do maintenance can you do it all? Some? Nothing at all?

There aren't any easy answers to what it will cost you to live your dream life aboard a boat, but we can supply some hard questions that will give you a realistic picture of costs. Get out a pencil and paper or start a new document on your computer.

First, make a complete list of where your money goes now. List everything, no matter how unrelated to your future life as a liveaboard. Some of the totals will surprise you; others will be relevant in ways you don't expect. List food, housing, insurance including annuities and long- term health care, time payments, obligations such as child support or eldercare, clothing costs averaged over a year or two, medical and dental costs averaged over two or three typical years, pet care, transportation, entertainment including subscriptions and cable TV, postage and Internet provider, savings, church and charity, dry cleaning, vacations, and so on.

We didn't say it would be easy. To make such as list, you have to go back through tax records, receipts and check stubs, review time payment obligations, and admit to yourself how much you've really been spending on spa treatments or shoes. When you are closer to moving aboard, you can cross out those items that will no longer apply, but don't be too quick with the blue pencil. If you decide to keep the house and rent it out, mortgage payments will continue and you'll have management and maintenance fees too. Check with a realtor or management company to get a dollar figure on what this service is likely to cost. Then put aside about 10% of the rent each month for repairs and replacements. They'll cost far more when you're not around to ride herd on things.

Some time payments will stop, of course: the car if you sell it, charge cards if you can ever get caught up, the mortgage if you sell the house. Don't forget, though, about the cemetery lots, the big-screen television, and payments on the boat itself.

Check off those expenses that won't change much after you move aboard. You'll eat and drink about the same (forget those dreams of living on fish and coconuts), buy newspapers and magazines, write to your friends, replace sheets and towels, fly home occasionally to see the family, continue charity giving, rent movies, and perhaps eat out much more than you presently do because that's part of the fun of cruising. You'll probably continue your life and health insurance and other policies that you will continue to need. Income taxes will continue if your income does.

Some expenses will drop or stop. If you've been dressing for a white collar job, you can stop buying suits and live in jeans. (It's easy, though, for a dedicated clothes horse to spend as much on designer jeans and sportswear as on business clothes.) Make-up, junk jewelry, three- martini lunches, and fads of all sorts fade for many liveaboards, but most of us continue our same, shore side spending addictions. Our friend Howard promised himself he'd quit smoking as soon as he quit his pressure-cooker job and moved aboard. Then he decided that commissioning the boat was a lot of pressure, but he'd quit when he finally get out into the islands. You can guess the ending. He never quit or cut down. In fact, smokes cost him more and more every year as cigarettes, taxes, and health costs continue to rise.

Cross out costs that will definitely stop: commuter tickets and tolls, home utilities, pool maintenance, subscriptions, and club dues (do, however, keep your yacht club membership because it can provide reciprocal privileges). If your legal address changes, you might also eliminate state sales taxes.

In revising your list now, you'll find yourself looking at painful decisions. Should you convert your group health insurance policy to a high-cost individual plan? Add a worldwide medical policy that flies you home if you're stricken on some godforsaken atoll? Will you keep your life insurance? Raise it? Continue supporting that charity that counts on your contribution year after year? Run out on child support or alimony? What about caring for a disabled sibling or your aging parents? A college fund for the children? Those fabulous gifts that are a family tradition at birthdays and Christmas?

Now, while you are still wrestling with costs, is a good time to face such decisions. Once you have moved aboard and thrown off the dock lines, problems become magnified. Fears about illness or debt are more overwhelming. Guilt over family duties is more pressing, regrets more unbearable, turning back more difficult. Make a stab at listing ballpark figures for these costs.

Continue your list with costs about which you can make an educated guess. If you don't yet have the boat, call a marine lender and find what it will cost per month for a 10-year-loan on a boat costing $100,000, a 15-year loan on a boat costing $250,000 or whatever. Call a few marinas to get an idea of nightly, monthly, and seasonal rates for a 35- or 50-footer, and ask what extra charges you might expect such as telephone hookup, electricity, cable television, and so on.

Some marinas also require proof of insurance. Even if you *think* you'll anchor out and live free forever, budget for marinas for the first year. Anchorages may not be as abundant or attractive as you think.

Next, call your insurer to learn what it will cost per year to insure the boat. If you already own the boat, you'll get an accurate picture of the cost of insuring that model at that age for the cruising area that will be your home. At the same time, ask what limits apply. You might, for example, have to stay within certain areas at certain times of the year. If you haven't yet bought a boat, a savvy marine insurer can tell you a great deal about ways you can save money by, say, opting for diesel power over gasoline or getting a trawler rather than a sailboat. All insurance companies have their own, funny quirks and prejudices. We once were canceled by a company that abruptly stopped covering sailboats for crossing the Gulf Stream, while continuing to cover power boats of any size or age for the same trip!

Talk to your insurer about a policy for the boat's contents. When everything you own is on board, you'll probably need special riders for the family silver, your stamp collection, computers, cameras, a library, and things that weekend boaters don't carry with them. You'll also need liability coverage for things that now come under your homeowner policy, e.g. your cat scratches a guest; your tennis ball gives somebody a black eye.

Call a couple of boatyards and ask the cost of hauling and bottom paint for your actual or mythical vessel. You'll need hauling at least once a year, perhaps twice. Look into mail order home school for your children, and factor in those costs plus extra for field trips to museums, extra book purchases, music lessons, art supplies, and perhaps some physical education such as trips to a gym or ballet lessons.

Well in advance, you can also learn the cost of mail forwarding and find the best deal on phone cards. If you will maintain your present address, you have an idea of what you'll pay in boat licensing and in state and local income taxes. If not, look into tax laws in Florida, California, Hawaii, or wherever your "home" base will be. Health and auto insurance are also predicated on your permanent address.

By now, a strong picture of your liveaboard costs is emerging and we go into the guesswork phase. This has two parts: new costs that come with the liveaboard life, and unexpected costs that nobody can predict.

New costs will include coin laundries, marine fuel (based on how many gallons your boat burns per hour and how many hours you plan to be underway each year), engine oil, generator fuels and maintenance, and ground transportation. This can be a big one, ranging from rental cars for major provisioning to native buses, sightseeing at each port you visit, maintaining a dinghy and outboard(s), and the cost of bicycles or mopeds that you carry along (they are high maintenance items in salt air) or rent in port. If you'll stay in one spot and will maintain a car, factor in the cost of its fuel, maintenance, insurance, and parking or garaging.

In a few categories, your liveaboard expenses will be somewhat higher than they are in your shore life, even with no change of consumption or lifestyle. Few countries in the world eat more economically than Americans do. In the West Indies or Europe, your food costs could double. Don't count on living off the land. Most land belongs to somebody. You could get fined or jailed for helping yourself. Fishing is time-intensive and is not always successful. And even in those nations where rice and produce are dirt cheap, other staples can be very costly. The more Americanized your diet, the more it will cost you to maintain it abroad.

In many categories (spare parts, food, incidentals) we often find ourselves paying higher prices because, as strangers in town, we don't know where to get the best deals. If you don't have a car for shopping around, or have to provision in small markets near the water, food costs soar. Thanks to the Internet, everything is available by mail, but shipping costs are going up every year. Medical and dental costs also rise for the roamer because most doctors and dentists charge more for your first visit. Yet, because you're on the go, you rarely see the same one twice. Add in the cost of medical, dental and eye care, pet care, and gift giving according to your past patterns.

From here on, we are flying blind. Nobody knows in advance what will break down, who will fetch up on a reef, how long the sails and engine will last, or what emergencies can throw your budget to the winds. Let's do some skylarking. Fuel costs depend on how far you plan to go, but the cruel truth is that we rarely meet a cruiser who spends as much time underway as planned. Friends are made. Maintenance has to be done. Docks are comfortable. Weather changes. Make a budget now for fuel and oil, then re-figure after a year of living aboard. Let's assume you'll be a fairly active cruiser. At intervals you will need to replace:

Charts

Everyone uses electronics these days, but they haven't entirely replaced paper charts, coast pilots, tide tables, cruising guides, guide books, nature guides, and foreign dictionaries.

Foul Weather Gear

You'll be lucky if it lasts five years. Good gear is expensive; cheap foul weather gear isn't worth buying.

Batteries

You can probably get three years out of your marine batteries. In addition to ship's batteries, you'll need others, some of them very costly.

Fuel and Oil

The more carefully you plan an itinerary, the more closely you can gauge fuel costs, but there's a lot of guesswork here. Don't assume, though, that you'll fly free just because yours is a sailboat. One couple with a 52-foot ketch told us they covered 7,124 miles in 265 days during which they ran the engine 572 hours (almost 10 percent of the time) and the generator 610 hours. They used 922 gallons of diesel fuel or 3.47 gallons per day. We figure that they got about 7.72 miles to the gallon for running and generating. Without the generator, they would have gotten about 16 miles to the gallon -- something to consider if you think that sailing means a free trip.

We did get through one entire year on 24 gallons, but only because we were willing to spend a lot of time becalmed. We find that most auxiliaries are used more than their owners admit. If you have a powerboat, of course, fuel use can be computed in advance. Don't forget to allow for generator fuel.

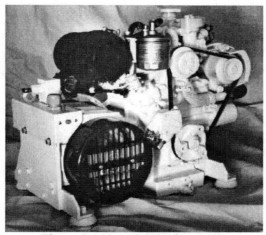

Figure 7-1 Next Generation Power

When trying to figure what the cost of cruising will be, don't forget the cost of fuel and oil for the generator.

Major Replacements

The life of your engine and other big-ticket parts of your boat depend greatly on how much you use them, how well you take care of them, and luck. As a rule of thumb, we recommend socking away about 5-10% per year of the cost of major replacements such as the engine, sails, standing rigging, generator, and so on. Some things may go 20-30 years. Others, such as upholstery, may not last longer than ten. Any monies that aren't needed can stay in your savings account, drawing interest and waiting for the day when you have a really backbreaking bill.

Minor Spares and Replacements

These are minor only in the since that you won't have to stock them on board if you live at the dock in the city. The more remote your cruising area, the more oddball your equipment, and the less time you can afford to languish in some port while you wait for parts, the more important it is for you to carry extensive spares such as engine bearings, valves, piston rings, valve guides, a piston, at least one injector, and all manner of ignition parts. In one year alone, we met four skippers who had lost their oil suddenly and burned out all their bearings.

The list of paint, rope, varnish, sandpaper, waxes, bilge cleaner, solvents and brushes is a mile long. You'll have a better idea of these ongoing costs after your first year of living aboard. Initial costs will be high; replacements will probably be less.

Purchases

No matter how complete your boat-home when you move aboard, there will be additional needs along the way. In his book *Blown Away*, Herb Payson said his family found it essential to have a second dinghy. Although you'll be shedding unneeded items after a few months of living aboard, you'll probably find a need for hundreds of dollars in small purchases . This category too is guesswork.

Services

If you can do everything aboard your boat, you'll spend little for mechanics, electricians, carpenters, and other marine service people. Even the handiest person, however, usually needs help with something and almost all of us have to be hauled by a boatyard. The more strict your budget, the more important to eliminate items that you can't maintain yourself.

Marine workers, at $20 and up, can bankrupt you. We have met all-thumbs boat owners who spend months in boat yards, and thousands of dollars, just to do barebones maintenance.

The Law and You

No matter how far we flee in our boats, taxes pursue us. The liveaboard who stays on the go, and keeps a low profile, may not catch the attention of state and local authorities but it's always smart to know what rules apply and to follow them. For example, a boat that stays in certain states' waters for six months may be subject to state taxes even though the boat is documented, or is licensed in another state. Many municipalities have harbor fees, limits on how long you can anchor, or a total prohibition on living aboard.

If you have a particular home port in mind, look into what state, county, and local taxes apply. Get the official story, then talk to other liveaboards about the *real* situation. There may be angles and wrinkles that make it better or worse than it appears. One big shock to people who move to Florida, which does not have an income tax, is an intangible assets tax that applies to stocks and bonds. Pay special attention to intangible taxes, state and local income taxes, the cost of licensing a boat, inheritance taxes, and real estate tax as it applies to liveaboards. In some states, you could find yourself unable to keep your boat-home and savings account if your spouse dies.

When you stand ready on the launch pad of your liveaboard life, what will your net worth be? The closer you are to leaving, the more accurate your figures will be, but here are some tips on adding up your net worth as of today. Keep in mind that we are talking net worth, not monthly income, which is another matter. For example, Social Security is not listed. It may have a value to you but only month by month depending on your age and your lifetime earnings. Since it has no lump sum value for the purposes of a net worth statement, it doesn't figure in this ledger. Get out a pad and pencil, and start a list.

The object is to come up with a figure that tells you what you would have in hand today if you liquidated everything. In amassing such a list can you get an overview of how independent you are, right now.

Ready Cash

In this column, list liquid assets plus other assets which are fairly well assured. These include bank accounts, money market funds, CD's, cash on hand, and monies you are fairly certain to collect soon (such as a maturing insurance policy or an IRS refund). Add in any sums you intend to have on hand on your upcoming takeoff date, if it's close at hand, such as a retirement bonus or lump sum settlement, IRA or Keogh, vested interest in a profit sharing or other retirement plan, insurance settlement, or maturing bonds or other investment.

Today's Value

In this column, you can list only what these items are worth today because they could be worth much more or less tomorrow. These include stocks, mutual funds, trusts, and tangible deposits such as silver bars or gold bullion. Add in the cash value of your life insurance policy (not the loan value). If you have a business partner, get a professional appraisal of what your share is worth on today's market. Add in the current market value of your car, boat, home (its fair market value, not your equity) and furnishings, and the garage sale value of items you could liquidate easily. The total will probably be impressive if yours is a typical household complete with appliances, yard care equipment, shop tools, electronics, sporting goods, and so on. If you don't have an inventory of these items, do one immediately because you'll need it to collect your insurance if your home burns down or is robbed. Now add in the value of valuables including jewelry, Oriental rugs, guns, sterling silver and china, antiques, art, furs, and collectibles of all kinds. Again, if you have no idea of their values, have them appraised and inventoried immediately. You'll need a professional appraisal to sell them at the best price, to insure them to carry with you, or to insure them if you leave them behind in storage.

The Debt Ledger

This is the tough part. Just when you thought you were riding high, you start listing your obligations. They include the balance due on your home mortgage, unpaid taxes, the unpaid balance on the cars and boat, the full balance due (not the monthly payment) on all credit cards, and the balance due on any other loans. Don't forget any lump sum payments that are coming up, such as a balloon payment, maturing of an auto lease, or a big annual real estate tax, college tuition, or insurance premium. If you have any debts to your broker, such as a margin account, list that too. If you have debts in partnership with someone else, don't forget them. If, for example, you have cosigned a note with one of your children, or have made bail for someone, you'll have that hanging over you until it is paid off or resolved. No matter how well intentioned you or the other party, something could go awry. You're now ready to subtract the little number from the big one to find out if you're ahead of the game, and how far.

By looking over the figures, you'll be better equipped to decide whether to sell the house or keep it, to use your available funds to pay off the RV or to keep making payments, or to sell the Oriental rugs and keep the coin collection. You can start making decisions about which assets to roll over, which to sell now (consider the tax consequences), and which to switch into assets that will contribute more income, more security, or more growth potential. When you're on the go full-time, it will be harder (and a lot less fun; you'll have better things to do) to keep abreast of financial dealings, the stock market, and shifting your funds constantly to squeeze another

1/4% of interest out of a CD. The time to start a strategy is now. And it begins with knowing just where, on the great fiduciary treadmill of life, you are trotting at this moment.

Chapter 8
Case Histories

Meet some current liveaboards and take inspiration from their stories.

Nick DiBlase

Via e-mail, Nick DeBlase wrote, "We live aboard our 1993, 52-foot Harbor Master in St. Clair Shores, MI. We purchased it used in Midland, Ontario (in 1998). Midland is at the bottom of Georgian Bay. Our trip bringing the boat back through almost 400 miles of four- and five-foot Great Lakes waves in windy September is a story in itself. Most people wonder how we heat in winter. We have two RV-style propane furnaces, one 40,000 BTU and one 20,000 BTU. We have a 100-gallon propane rank that sits on the dock and is refilled every 3-5 weeks depending on the weather. Cost is about $145 (in year 2000 dollars) per fill-up.

As Nick wrote, the temperature outdoors was 2 degrees and he was a comfortable 72 degrees inside his houseboat. "There is nothing like living aboard," he enthuses.

Pete's Story

Pete e-mailed us that he has been living on his Stardust houseboat for six years on Lake Conroe in Texas. . He bought the boat in salvage condition and named it *Resurrection* after rebuilding her from the hull up to a crisp, new 26-foot Bimini top. He tells us we couldn't recognize the boat now from what she was, and he loved every minute of the redo. He's now 58 years old and retired, while his son runs his business. Thirty years ago, he had 10 heart attacks and two, open-heart surgeries, but he and his wife credit living aboard, not the operations, with saving his life.

The Pitts Family

Steven and Catherine Pitts and their cat, Muffy, live aboard their Heritage West Indies 30-footer, a Charlie Morgan-designed-and-built center-cockpit sloop. When we heard from them last they were docked at Merritt Island, FL, where Steven was commuting to Celebration, FL and working as a technical writer for Disney Cruise Line. Catherine works aboard the boat, telecommuting for IBM.

Figure 8-1 Steven Pitts

Steven Pitts turned a fire-damaged charter boat into a comfortable home.

Their glass-reinforced plastic boat was built in 1977 and they picked it up in 1988 for $14,000 because of fire damage. Steve replaced all the wiring and plumbing, and turned a former charter boat into a two-person home. Thanks to their "15-minute rule" they can always get away from the dock in 15 minutes or less when they have a notion to put to sea. Catherine's office was designed to stay put, so it doesn't have to be stowed at the end of the day.

The couple cook on a three-burner propane stove with oven, a propane grill, and a small microwave. Their small AC refrigerator can be run on shore power or on a 600W inverter, running about 30 minutes out of every hour and drawing about 5 amps. In the future they plan to pay off their bills and set sail for the Bahamas, Gulf of Mexico, and the Caribbean.

Merle and Mary Quigley

The couple started weekend boating in New Jersey for about five years, then cruised the Hudson River and lived aboard in Rockland County NY for two winters and three summers. Then they went back to cruising the New Jersey coast for five years. Now docked in Brooklyn, they are still living aboard. "We're year-round liveaboards in the frozen north," Mary e-mailed us. As she wrote, she was looking out at six inches of new snow, a snowstorm that was turning to hail. On the dock, drifts were up to two feet high. Yet their 46-foot Chris Craft was cozy warm with its fireplace and forced air heating throughout the vessel. The couple, who used to live in the Chelsea area of Manhattan, find their boat more modern and commodious. They have an electric barbecue built into their galley countertop and they redid the head with a six-foot whirlpool tub with a shower. Merle is retired and Mary, a New York City administrator, is on sick leave from her job.

"I love living aboard winter, summer, spring and fall," she says. "Of course I encounter all kinds of comments and reactions when other women hear about my nontraditional way of life. Still, what can I say but 'Don't knock it until you've tried it.' The good certainly out weights the bad. I like to ask people if they like to go to the shore, then remind them that I get to go every day."

Gary Whitson

He calls himself Banjerman (after a banjo, not after the Dutch-built boat) and intends to live aboard his houseboat six months of the year after he retires in about 2004. "My wife and I plan to take her from Knoxville to Mobile on the Tenn-Tom Waterway, taking our time getting there and just kinda lazing along. I guess you could call me a Huck Finn. I've read that book 25- 30 times, I guess, and it's about time I read it again. It has been my lifelong dream to take a long trip on the rivers and I hope to make it happen at least once."

Looking Back

Known only as "barb henry" or punkin@inter-linc.net, a woman e-mailed us that the first edition of this book, which was published by Hearst, was the first book she bought when she and her husband bought their houseboat in Sacramento CA. "It was a great help to us," she writes. "We had embarked on a life we knew nothing about. We lived on our 42-foot houseboat on the Sacramento and Feather rivers. It was the best time of my life and I never go a day without wishing I was aboard again. We're now divorced and I don't know anyone who ever understands the world of living on a houseboat. Nonetheless, it's where I long to be." Our guess is that there about two million men who would give their eye teeth to meet a gal who loves living aboard as much as Punkin does!

Annie and Bob Bolderson

On our list of role models, the Boldersons are in the

Top Ten. By the time we arrived on the scene, they were experienced liveaboards. They took possession of *Nymph Errant,* their 46- foot schooner, at Gibson Island in 1964 and sailed her south to Fort Lauderdale to refit her for charter service. The name was from a Noel Coward play that was popular about the time she was built (1939) and her history included participation in the evacuation of Dunkirk in World War II. As they arrived at their dock in Fort Lauderdale, her ancient auxiliary died.

By the time they had refitted the boat and had all their inspections and government paperwork in hand, they were almost fully booked for a season of chartering in the Bahamas. "It was the heyday for crewed, offshore sailing charters in the islands," Annie remembers now. "We all must have thought it would go on forever...none of us had thoughts of chucking it all to go back ashore."

The schooner had two double cabins forward, each with a head, and the main salon could convert to sleep two more guests. Bob had a bunk on the port side aft, where they stowed the mattress that Annie put atop the top-loaded freezer, where she slept. "I took a lot of ribbing about that," she remembers now, recalling nine happy years as a successful charter couple.

We don't recall anyone working as hard as the Boldersons did, keeping their schooner in beautiful condition while giving their guests the vacation of a lifetime. Annie is a consummate cook; both are superb hosts. Meals were often decided at the last minute, depending on what came up on the end of the spear. Annie's side dishes, salads and homemade desserts, plus the catch of the day, became island legends. (The story about them in the *New York Times* covered more than half a page).

They loved the mix of charter guests, locals, and other yachties. One family, Annie recalls, had their children with them. After dinner, Mom threw the iron skillet overboard. The first job the boys had the next morning was to dive in to the bottom, rescue the skillet, scrub it with sand, and bring it back aboard in time for breakfast.

The Webb Family

 Christopher and Tricia Webb met while in college after she enrolled in a sailing course. He was more interested in her than in the sailing, and he got the girl. They married and moved aboard a 27-foot sailboat, with their dog, in 1983 in Ventura, CA. The next year they bought a 39-foot kit boat that wasn't quite half finished and moved aboard while working on it. Their son Joshua was born in 1985 and by 1989 they were able to quit their jobs and go sailing for five months. They headed south and almost two years later were in Texas via the Panama Canal and Florida. Their daughter was born in 1993 and in 1997, they sailed for the Bahamas.

Figure 8-2 Chris Webb

Chris and Tricia Webb, Megan and Joshua, live aboard their 51-footer. They left in March, 2000 for the next leg of the journey that had begun in California and took them through the Panama Canal to Florida.

 The 39-footer was getting smaller as the children grew, so the family moved into a 51-foot Morgan that the family worked on for more than a year before setting sail again in March, 2000 for points unknown.

 "After 17 years of living aboard, a few thoughts come

to mind," muses Christopher. "When first moving aboard, give it time. There is a huge learning curve...not the same as a two-week vacation or charter. During much of our time aboard, I have been working on boats and haven't needed suits, but Tricia works in the medical profession, so she needs a wardrobe."

He says if he had it to do over, he wouldn't tackle a major building project because it means all work and no sailing. Despite the stories in the glossy periodicals, he finds that most builders never finish and go sailing. "It's far easier to work hard at a good paying job, buy a completed boat, and enjoy her," declares Webb. Living aboard has been good environment for raising our children." The couple choose their marinas carefully, searching for places that had other liveaboards. "The friendships we have formed and the quality of life are far better than any we have found ashore."

The Webbs also tackled home schooling, which allows them to be more involved with and provide a better education for their children than they feel can be found in public schools.

Ken and Valerie Waine

The Waines are a husband-wife team who make a living with their boat-home by chartering by the day or week out of Marathon in the Florida Keys. Ken is a licensed captain, Valerie provides the lifestyle, gourmet meals, and planning. Their home base is a marina on the ocean side of Marathon, giving them breathtaking sunset views and easy access to Hawk Channel or the Bahamas when they put to sea. On "vacation", they may go as far as the Virgin Islands, Turks and Caicos, Puerto Rico, or Dominican Republic. After ten years on board, they are still enthusiastic about living aboard.

Figure 8-3 Ken and Valerie Waine

Ken and Valerie Waine live aboard their yacht Latigo, which they charter by the day or week.

Don and Sue Moesly

Two more of our Top Ten are Don and Sue Moesly, whom we first met when we were anchored near each other in the Bahamas. We had caught a big bull dolphin and had no refrigeration, so we had plenty to share with the neighbors. We have been friends, ashore and afloat, ever since. Don is a professional wood finisher, whose shore business is refinishing fine woods and restoring antiques. Sue, a fellow Buckeye, is also a fellow writer.

Sue's two-volume book *Circumnavigation: Sail the Tradewinds* (Wescott Cove Publishing Company) is the consummate guide for sailing around the world with the trades. They spent five years aboard their 38-foot, double-ended wooden ketch *Svea,* living the life of ultimate freedom that others only dream about. In total harmony with nature and each other, the couple love watching birds at sea. "On the 47-day voyage from Cape Town to Bequia, when I said we were going home to Fort Lauderdale, I realized that we *were* home. Our boat was home." The couple are now restoring a 46-foot Pan Oceanic cutter that will "take us back to the sea we love."

Figure 8-4 Don Moesly

Don and Sue Moesly did one five-year circumnavigation and they are equipping yet another boat to go back to sea.

John Kaufman

John Kaufman is typical of the many entrepreneurs who have found a way to have it all -- a boat, the cruising life, and a business. He started boating as a seven-year-old boy in central Pennsylvania, progressing as most of us do from smaller to larger. For his 40th birthday, his gift to himself was to leave the upper Chesapeake and point the bow southward. Living now aboard his 42-foot motoryacht, *Ship Happens*, he has cruised thousands of miles up and down the Intracoastal Waterway.

It took a two-year break from nonstop cruising to establish his Bristol Fashion Publications but now everything is in place and he's off again, operating his business by telephone and e-mail. "I plan to stay on the water until someone has to slide me over the side," he says now.

"I've always thought it strange to hear another cruiser, when asked where they are headed, to say 'We're headed home.' When I'm on my boat I am home. I never keep a slip when I leave an area because I never know if I'll want to come back. There may be an area I like more."

What is Kaufman's advice for new liveaboard cruisers? "Don't keep a schedule or itinerary," he urges. "As often as I have traveled the waterway, it still amazes me to hear people on the radio with a long list of times and dates they MUST be somewhere for some reason. I have also witnessed bad decisions, resulting in damaged boats and people, when somebody had to be somewhere regardless of the weather. Take it slow, enjoy whatever an area has to offer," he suggests. "You'll get to where you think you have to be someday, if you still want to go."

"The people I have met on the water, over nearly forty years, have been some of the best people I have ever known. It is hard for me to imagine living anywhere other than aboard my boat, for a house is nothing more than a poorly built boat that doesn't move."

Figure 8-5   John Kaufman & Bo

John and Bo have traveled thousands of Intracoastal Waterway miles together, aboard Ship Happens.

Chapter 9
Fitting It All In

A list of all the items that need to be stowed in a liveaboard vessel sounds like a household inventory plus a commissioning list for the QEII. You'll probably carry the Christmas decorations, income tax records going back several years, out-of-season clothes, the sewing machine, tools and spares to fix everything aboard, a library of books and music, and hobby needs for every member of the family. You'll need not just everyday galley gear but extras for company and perhaps equipment to can or preserve, package and freeze, or dehydrate foods required for your travels. You need not just clothing and linens for a couple of weeks, but for a year-round life, with plenty of spares for those times when you can't do the laundry. You'll also need fuel, water, and provisions for weeks and even months.

Stowage solutions begin in the showroom. Before you buy the boat, open every door and drawer to inventory how much storage space is really available. Huge areas, you will find, are already filled with tanks, wiring, pumps, ducts, pipes, and other behind-the-scenes space stealers.

The stowage situations most commonly overlooked include:

Dinghies

A dinghy is essential to getting around anchorages and

into shoals and gunkholes. It helps you sent anchors, and take soundings of tricky harbors before you venture in with the big boat. It's your work platform for painting the topsides, and it may also serve as your lifeboat. It takes you fishing, and "next door" to have drinks with your anchorage neighbors. If there are two or more people aboard your boat, with different interests or schedules, you may need two dinghies just as some families need two cars.

Figure 9-1

Figure 9-2 Porta-Bote International

If you don't have room to carry a dinghy, consider getting a boat that folds and stows in a long, thin package, or an inflatable that deflates to stow in a round, fat package.

Our first dink was a fiberglass pram, and friends warned us that we would lose it eventually if we towed it. However, there simply wasn't room on board. So we *did* tow it and we *did* lose it after two years. By then inflatables were affordable, tough, and reliable, and we replaced the pram with the Avon that we still have. It's small enough when deflated to carry on deck, is stable enough to use as a swim platform -- it's easily boarded from the water -- and it doesn't bang up the hull when it is tied alongside. With a CO_2 cartridge carried for emergencies, it can be partially inflated in seconds for use as a life raft. During heavy rains when we hadn't had a freshwater bath in months, we let it fill with water and used it as a big bathtub.

On the minus side, it's a production to get the boat inflated when we get into a harbor and want to get to the beach, and an even greater project to deflate, clean, dry, and stow it before getting underway again. Inflatables are beasts to tow and row and, unless you use floorboards, which add weight and bulk to the overall package you must stow, it's difficult to move around inside and to find a dry spot to stow groceries.

You have many decisions to make about a dinghy: inflatable or rigid, powered or oared or sail, the size, the quality, and whether to carry it in davits or tow it astern using lines or towing whips. Whatever your choice, it will be your town car, SUV, station wagon, and bass boat. Choose yours, and its stowage method, with care.

Sails and Dock Lines

They are enormously bulky and fractious, yet it's essential that they be kept handy for immediate use. They're usually wet when you bring them in. So, if you need to stow them below, you want them kept separate from living areas of the boat. If the boat doesn't have a dedicated sail locker, don't forget that they can fill your entire forepeak or lazarette. The same can be said for a rope locker. Stowage for the anchor rodes, by contrast, is usually designed into the boat.

His, Hers, and Ours

Aboard our 29-foot sloop, our living quarters were small compared to what most other liveaboards have, yet we never quibble about stowage spaces that are his alone or hers alone. It's important that everyone have spaces to fill with whatever is important to him or her, without someone questioning why you need all that junk or what are you going to do with THAT, for crying out loud. Every liveaboard has to work out an individual system. Generally, everything abaft the companionway was his for tools, snorkel gear, spares, sails, and extra anchors. Without disturbing the galley, Gordon could do almost any maintenance or repair job on the boat, or load all the gear into the dinghy for fishing, diving, shopping, or a beach expedition.

Janet's turf was the galley and most other areas below. Equipment for writing was kept in one area; Gordon's photography department was in another. Charts, books and music tapes, and the hanging locker were "ours". We each had a small, net hammock in the forepeak, where we slept, for other clothes and reading material. We could have as many magazines as we liked, as long as they fit into our personal space. When Christmas came, weeks after our last shopping port, we were always able to pull out a few surprises for each other.

Divide and Conquer

When you are in the showroom and see a huge stowage bin under a bunk or settee, it looks like Mammoth Cave. In use, however, it turns into a mammoth jumble because what you want is always on the bottom. Rather than trying to put permanent dividers into large bins, lockers, and unused berths (which are great stowage areas), we found it best to use removable compartments in manageable sizes. The marketplace today offers such a wonderful choice of plastic containers, it's possible to fine-tune each storage area to the utmost for only a few dollars in K-Mart plastics.

Plastic "milk carton" carriers are easily handled, are sturdy enough to stack several layers deep even when filled with canned foods, and they are filled with holes, so they are ideal for things that need to drain or air. Plastic dish pans are inexpensive and attractive to use as "drawers" filled with folded towels, the sewing kit, and other oddments. They have no lid, but are fine to use one layer deep in shallow spaces. Each of us used a dishpan as a personal drawer for toiletries.

Speaking of toiletries, it may be better for each crew member to have a personal, portable toilet kit that can be grabbed to go into whatever head is empty on the boat, or into the marina shower, as needed. If you use different facilities often, it's better to stay portable than to allocate stowage space for everything in the seagoing version of a medicine cabinet. We prefer the type of toilet kit that hangs from one hook and unfolds to present an entire closet of toiletries. Rarely do marina bathrooms have a clean, dry place to spread out your gear, towel, and clean clothes. If you're lucky, though, you'll probably have a hook or two, or at last a nail to hang things on. You'll be glad for a toilet kit that needs only that.

Lidded plastic containers are available in every size from half pint (safety pin, paper clips, rubber bands) to the giant size made for use in the bed of a pickup truck. Some have press-tight lids and are watertight. Other styles have a lid that locks on. They're about as waterproof as you can get. They're good for storing dry foods, the first aid kit, and an extra set of clothes and bedding for emergencies. They are pretty much fail-safe except for mice and rats, which can chew through plastic, and mildew, which can thrive if dampness gets locked in. We also use inexpensive plastic containers as dividers inside galley drawers, to bring a little order to the general jumble.

In choosing these containers, it's good to have measurements with you. We look for styles that are rectangular or square rather than round, are stackable if possible, are flexible and strong (rather than brittle, as clear plastic shoe boxes are), and which have the most usable space. Some are molded with far more space efficiency than others.

Fishing supply stores and catalogs offer a huge choice of portable tackle boxes, which can also be used to separate and stow nuts and bolts, hobby or sewing supplies, and other small items. If you have an area where one can be built in, look for models that have a flange and door and are meant to be mounted permanently in a hole cut in a deck or bulkhead.

Closet supply departments and catalogs carry two types of plastic storage bags that allow for air evacuation. One type has a fitting that accepts a vacuum cleaner hose. Fill it with blankets or other bulky items that you want to stow for a while, suck out the air, and you've halved the size. This type is fairly waterproof. The other type, suitable for sweaters and other small items, has a one-way valve through which air is forced out as you press or roll the filled bag. This type is watertight, but not waterproof, and eventually air leaks back in.

While in the closet supply aisle, look for zippered garments bags large enough to hold one or two suits or dresses. Fabric bags are preferable to plastic, which doesn't breathe. Place one dress-up outfit in a separate bag to keep it safe from the general jostling. Tubular plastic hangers are about the smoothest and most practical to use on board. Wood hangers with metal parts can rust, and any roughness in the wood will snag and wear clothes as the boat moves. One rough spot in a hanger can chew through a garment in only a few days underway. Be sure to sand out any rough spots in the hanging locker interior too.

Heavy mesh bags are perfect for stowing great wads of stuff such as the laundry, dive and snorkel gear, and engine rags. If you use marina showers, get a mesh bag for each family member for carrying a bath towel, washcloth, change of clothes, and anything else that is too large to fit in a personal toilet kit. Small stuff bags, purchased or made on your home sewing machine from a sturdy fabric such as duck or denim, help divide up a stowage hammock. Use one for socks, another for undies, and so on. You might color code them by item or by family member -- camouflage for Junior, pink gingham for Sis, and so on. If you're sewing your own, add a couple of pockets on the outside to hold small items.

When the heel or toe wears out of socks, cut off the ribbed tops and use them as bands to hold rolled sun hats, sweaters, and other springy items that tend to take on a life of their own when in your clothing drawer or hammock. We also use them as "bottle booties" on glass bottles and jars to keep them from clanking together and breaking. Even though we use a lot of home- canned meat in glass jars, we've never had one break underway. These sock tops are washable but, when they get grotty, there is a never-ending new supply as old socks continue to wear out.

Classified Stowage

Only you can decide how to pile things in so you'll always know where to find a new bag of flour or a can of pumpkin pie filling. We like to keep one food locker as a "ready" locker filled with things that are used often, such as spices and condiments, plus one can each of meat, sauce, vegetable and fruit. If a hurry-up meal is needed in a seaway, you can always throw a few cans in the pressure cooker with rice, and create a meal.

In larger stowage bins, we try to keep canned meats together in one section, vegetables in another, fruit, soups, and miscellaneous sauces and condiments in a separate section. With one glance, it's easy to tell if you're running low on one or another. Even in the driest boat, some provision should be made for protecting and labeling cans. They can be sprayed with clear lacquer, or plastic bagged. Some sailors like to remove the labels and mark cans with a grease pencil. In a flooding accident, any labels that come off turn to papier maché and clog bilge pumps.

Flour and other dry foods should be wrapped and

stowed in the driest area available. The smaller the boat, the more important it is to stow heavier things lower and lighter foods, such as paper products, higher, to avoid upsetting the boat's handling.

In addition to "ready" storage and "dead" stowage, we found areas we called "dead- dead." By taking out drawers and delving deep into corners and under floorboards, we found lots more storage space. It was awkward to get into, but roomy and welcome. On long cruises, we filled these spaces with items for re-supply later. At the other end of the spectrum was temporary storage consisting of one or two brown paper grocery bags that were crammed in any place handy. They were filled with store-bought bread, puffy snacks and perishable fruit just before we left port on a long cruise. Within a few days, the foods were gone and the bags discarded. Meanwhile, we hadn't gone to the trouble of stowing foods that would be gone or inedible within a few days.

If you'll be cruising from one foreign port to another, you'll also need a lockable locker for bonded stores. This allows you to buy duty-free items, such as liquor, which must be locked up until you leave that port.

Stow It and Secure It

There is nothing more disconcerting to the new liveaboard than to have a neat, smoothly running, floating household that comes completely unglued the first time a little wake hits the boat. Even well-stowed supplies can come loose in big seas. Experienced liveaboards may go for years without trouble until the day the Ultimate Wave pries loose things that had never budged before. We experienced such a whammy while crossing the Gulf Stream with Janet's father on board. As she scrambled to gather up books and junk that had never broken loose, he kept muttering, "My poor little girl, my poor little girl."

The first step is to appreciate the monstrous forces at

work. In even a slight heel, canned foods can shift against a locker door and break through unless the lock is a good one. Unless you'll be in only the tamest waters, get the strongest, marine quality latches and hinges. A wood toggle is cheap and easy to make, easy to unlock and lock, and it's strong.

If you have countertop items (microwave oven, toaster oven) they should be screwed down or well secured using marine fittings. Book shelves need sturdy wood slats. Shock cord isn't enough to hold things in high seas. Neither is florist clay, although it is a popular stick- down for small, light, decorative items. Most seagoing liveaboards build in special holders for bottles and other breakables. We once toured a Feadship that carries an entire set of Waterford crystal glasses, each with its own nest. Such holders take up a lot of space, though, so our answer was to use the bottle booties and to alternate plastic bottles with glass ones so glass wouldn't clink against glass. These days, it's possible to buy almost everything, including liquor, in plastic bottles except down-island, where rum is still bottled in glass.

If your dinghy is carried right-side up, it needs a sturdy cover with a ridge pile to shed water. Otherwise, a rogue wave could fill it suddenly with water, tripling its weight, and jerking it loose from its lashings. If it's carried upside down, the dinghy should be held down with sturdy fastenings. The same goes for all other deck equipment including PWCs and dock boxes.

Finding space is half the battle. The rest is finding what you need when you need it, and keeping it all from coming UN-stowed when the going gets rough.

Storage Solutions

Figure 9-3 Gordon Groene

This galley has dedicated storage for dishes of each size, which are held securely.

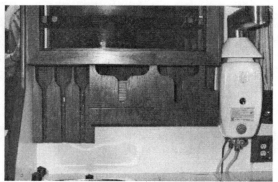

Figure 9-4 Gordon Groene

Note the cutouts that hold stacked glasses and plates securely, and the bulkhead-mounted water heater, which heats water only as needed.

Figure 9-5

One way to secure appliances is with a tambour door that operates much like a roll-top desk.

Figure 9-6 Davis Instruments

This ditty bag attaches anywhere for temporary stowage of small items.

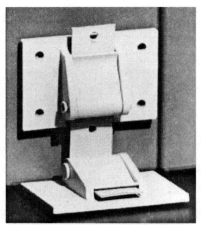

Figure 9-7 Fastening Solutions Inc.

It's essential that countertop items be well secured. Found in marine and RV stores, this T-6 fastener is said to hold up to 1,300 pounds.

Figure 9-8 Illinois Tool Works

Coated wire shelving provides secure storage with good air circulation.

122

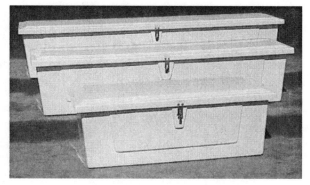

Figure 9-9 Better Way Products Inc.

Dock boxes can be installed on deck to expand your storage and add a seat.

Figure 9-10 Stuffed-Shirt Company

A toilet kit that hangs from one hook is ideal for marina showers because there is rarely space to spread out your toiletries, towels, and change of clothes.

Chapter 10
Cash Flow on the Go

It was like culture shock, except that we were still in our native land. We were accustomed to driving up to the bank window, handing over a check, and getting in return a deposit slip, some cash, a cheerful hello, and a bone for the dog. All that changed when we arrived in Fort Lauderdale, where everyone seemed to assume we had come to pull off the Brinks job of the century. The cashier's check we'd brought to bankroll our fitting-out was refused by the bank, and our traveler's checks were refused by a discount superstore. Our world had turned upside down!

It is a tremendous help that national ATM networks now allow us to get cash almost anywhere, but it still takes time for the new liveaboard to deal with the practical problems of being a stranger everywhere one goes. To balance the rebuffs, there will be many kindnesses.

We found that a passport makes the best ID, far better than an out-of-state driver's license. We also learned not to let our cash reserves get too low, to shop around for the best deals in banking and savings, to use electronic deposit where possible, and to use credits cards with a cash-back advantage for every purchase where cards are accepted. We use them for all fuel and food, Internet goods and services, and even for some medical and dental bills. Even our telephone calling card charges go to a credit card. At the end of each year, we get a kickback of about $150 from our Discover card alone. It carries no annual fee and, because we pay the bill in full each month, we don't care how high an interest rate it charges.

One of our favorite ways to carry safe and available cash in the States continues to be U.S. Savings Bonds. Unlike traveler's checks, they can be purchased free and they earn interest until they are cashed in. On the minus side, they can be cashed only at participating banks and they must be held for a minimal period of several months before they can be redeemed at all. Too, they aren't good outside the United States, not even in foreign branches of American banks.

Dan Pederson, author of U.S. Savings Bonds, reminds savers that $3 billion in bonds is being held after they no longer earn interest. It can mean "thousands of dollars" in lost return on your money, warns Pederson. Included are all bonds issued in and before April, 1958, and between December and April, 1968. "The ultimate winners," says Pederson," are bond owners who keep accurate records of their bonds and treat them with the same scrutiny they give their other assets." For a free brochure and record keeping sheet from The Savings Bond Informer, call (800) 927-1901. Pederson's web site is www.bondinformer.com.

We try to get by with as little cash outlay as possible. In paying for any goods or service, we try the bonus-paying credit cards first. Why use cash, which costs you money to get from an ATM, or a debit card, which debits your account immediately, when you can use a credit card that has a 25-day float and a year-end bonus? Our second choice is to use a personal check, which is almost always accepted for marina rent and professional services. Checks are also used for paying bills by mail. (Free checking is available from many banks. You may have to be over age 55 or maintain a minimum balance in a CD.) Only as a last resort do we part with cash.

When you move aboard and go cruising, there is no point in staying with your hometown bank. Shop ruthlessly for the best deal on checking, CDs, brokerage, IRAs, and so on. It can be done on the Internet. If you don't want to bank online, use the Web just for comparison shopping.

Accounts   and   monies   can   be   moved   around electronically. The goods you have in your safe deposit box cannot. Two warnings are in order. In some states, a safety deposit box is sealed if one party dies. Even though everything in the box belongs to you, it could be tied up for months in such states if your other signatory dies. You also don't want a large checking or savings account in a state where such accounts are frozen when one party dies. The second problem for the liveaboard is that banks do not insure the contents of safe deposit boxes. If that is where you are stashing your personal Fort Knox, look into private insurance.

Credit cards, for all their merits, are a mixed blessing. It's very costly to use them to get a cash advance because there is usually an up-front fee in addition to interest, which is charged from Day One. Even if you pay the balance in full each month, you'll pay a fortune in interest and penalties if your mail is delayed and you are late in paying the bill. Some credit card companies allow you to pay in advance even if you haven't received the bill. During times when your mail might be delayed, keep track of all receipts and send a check for what you owe.

One more warning to worldwide cruisers. In this country, you may have only a minor inconvenience or an added fee or penalty for using a card over your credit limit but, in some countries, it is a felony to try to use a maxed-out card. You could end up in a Third World jail. Keep track of your charges.

Credit cards have one more benefit that most people don't know about. When you are dealing with a small merchant who accepts credit cards, ask if you'd get a discount if you pay cash. Often, it works because the merchant gets his money right now, and without having to pay the credit card cut of about 4%. And he or she usually accepts a check; it doesn't have to be real cash. Even if you get only the 4% discount, both you and the merchant are ahead. In some cases, we score an even better discount. Just don't try this unless you are dealing with the business principal. Clerks and underlings aren't authorized to make deals.

There are other ways to get cash on the go. One is to have it wired to you. A friend takes the cash to a Western Union office and gives them your name plus information on how to reach you when it arrives. The cost varies with the amount sent and the destination. Charges are high, but the money arrives within hours. Money can also be sent with a USPS money order. Don't expect a small post office to have hundreds of dollars on hand, however. If you're in a real hurry, have the M.O. sent by Express Mail.

There are two Express Mail services, so don't be confused by them. One reaches you at the marina or other street address; the other comes to your nearest post office. Just don't use a post office box for Federal Express. If you want to take a chance on mailing negotiable wealth including cash, coins, gold bars and Treasure Bills, send them via Registered Mail. It's kept under lock and key, and every person who handles this mail must sign for it, so it isn't the fastest way but it is the safest. And it can be insured. Don't confused it with Certified Mail, which is cheaper but merely establishes proof of delivery. It offers no other protection.

If you're going to be in one port long enough, it can be a convenience to open at least a small bank account there. You can deposit checks and have access to the money after they clear. It's also easier to pass checks locally if they are on a local bank. Know what bank charges and state laws apply. Some banks charge for inactive accounts. In some states, accounts that are inactive for a certain period revert to the state. When you move on, close the account.

One other account was invaluable to us. We opened a joint account with Janet's parents back in New York. To avoid complications, the amount was kept low. When we were out of the country, the folks could deposit checks that came in and draw out monies to pay postage for forwarding our mail. If we wanted to send a gift, or send flowers for a family funeral, Mom could draw on our "friendly account" to take care of things. If the balance got too high, we could transfer money to our own account. If it got too low, we simply sent a check to fatten it. Money couldn't buy the help we were getting from the folks in terms of mail forwarding and other things, but the "friendly account" did mean that they weren't out of pocket.

When you're cruising out of your home country, things get more complicated. When you use a charge card, your account is charged the exchange rate that applies on the day the merchant turns in the bill for your purchase or restaurant meal. Sensing a big move, the merchant could choose to delay turning in the charge until a more favorable rate applies. Still, we like using credit cards because ATMs are very costly to use overseas. There's a big charge and the least favorable exchange rate. Credit charges, by contrast, usually get the most favorable exchange.

Before leaving your home country, look into getting an ATM card that is in widespread, international use. We once spent half a day with some Americans on a Caribbean island who were desperately looking for an ATM that would accept their card, which was well known in the U.S. but unknown here. They never did find one. Second, find out what PIN number applies to your card abroad. It may have more or fewer digits that are required at home. When changing money abroad, you'll get the best rates at banks, never at hotels, restaurants, shops, and ATMs. If you're carrying traveler's checks, get an internationally-known brand such as American Express or Barclay's. Buy in denominations of at least $100 or $500 because many nations charge a tax on each transaction. To use four $25 checks, you'll pay four times more tax than if you cash one check at $100.

If you want to lock in an exchange rate before you go, get traveler's checks in foreign currency. They can be found at www.foreignexchange.com and other Internet sites. Any time you're cashing a traveler's check, don't sign it until you're sure it will be accepted. Then countersign it in the presence of the merchant. Incidentally, make sure your original signature, when you first purchase the checks, is indelible and that the pen is not an erasable ball point. Some cruisers have been burned when their traveler's checks were stolen, erased, then re-signed and cashed by the bad guys.

If you'll be spending a lot of money overseas -- buying a boat there, for instance -- arrange with your bank for an international letter of credit.

No matter where you're cruising, keep abreast of money trends. If you're stuck with too many Euros or EC dollars or rubles, you could find them worth far less than you paid for them, especially in trying to exchange them outside their home country. For example, we remember a time when the Bahamian dollar traded on a par with the U.S. dollar inside the Bahamas, but you couldn't get a fraction of that if you tried to exchange them back into greenbacks when you got home. Keep track of interest rates, which could sink or rise wildly. We've met liveaboards whose funds were tied up at 3-4% when they could have been getting triple that. When your boat is filled with canned goods, it's easy to forget about interest rates, exchange rates, and the price of pork belly futures. Still, the piper must be paid at some time, and you need to stay one jump ahead of things.

Take Credit

It's a nightmare scenario. You're cruising somewhere when you need a job, a new credit card, new insurance policy, or a loan, and you suddenly find that your name is mud. How can you check your credit rating to make sure people are getting accurate information about you? If your credit is bad, how can you correct it?

"Give yourself a credit check," advises Donald Elder of the Federal Trade Commission. The FTC's publication, "Credit Repair: Help Yourself First" warns consumers about the many scam artists who say they can erase your bad credit or remove a bankruptcy or lien from your record. If you're in hot water financially, the FTC suggests that you may be the best person to get yourself out of it. Request a copy of Best Sellers, a list of FTC publications from Consumer Response Center, Federal

Trade Commission, Washington DC 20580.

Even if you don't have credit problems or a bad credit record, it's a good idea for the liveaboard to conduct a credit check up in advance to make sure there won't be unpleasant surprises on the road ahead. Three of the largest companies that issue such reports are Experian (formerly TRW), Box 949, Allen, TX, tel. (800) 682-7654; Equifax, Box 740, Atlanta, GA 30374, tel. (800) 685-1111 and Trans Union, Box 390, Springfield, PA 19064, tel. (800) 916-8800.

Your rights under the Fair Credit Reporting Act include:

* You are entitled to a free copy of your credit report if you have been denied credit, insurance or employment and request the report within 60 days after you receive notice of the denial. You're entitled to one free report a year if (1) you are unemployed and plan to seek work within 60 days, (2) you are on welfare or (3) your report is inaccurate because of fraud. Otherwise, a credit bureau charges up to $8 for a copy of your report, which is cheap insurance against future surprises like those described above:

If you are denied credit, insurance or employment, the company where you applied must give you the name and address of the reporting credit bureau.

Ask the credit bureau for a dispute form and submit it, with supporting documentation, to clear your name. There is no charge to correct mistakes that were not your fault.

Be aware that if you went bankrupt within the last 10 years, it stays on your record. Second, information about a lawsuit or judgment against you can be reported for seven years or until the statute of limitation expires, whichever is longer. Third, information reported because of an application for a job with a salary of $75,000 or more has no time limit. Nor does information reported because of an application for more than $150,000 worth of credit or life insurance.

If a "credit repair" company claims it can remove the above items from your file, or create a new credit identity or social security number for you, you may be committing fraud.

Rate.Net

If you have trouble keeping up with the best interest rates while you're cruising , try www.rate.net to find out what institutions are paying the best for savings accounts, CDs and jumbos. The service also tells who is charging lowest rates for loans and insurance.

Chapter 11
Mail Call

The electronic revolution has been an enormous boon to liveaboards, who now have the same, easy, cheap access to e-mail as anyone else. Still, most of us need an address where we can receive real mail, bills, letters from family and friends who are not online, magazines, catalogs, and all the other communications minutiae that put us fully in touch with our world. If you live in a paperless world, skip this chapter. For ourselves, we've been online for some years, but the U.S. Mail is still an important part of our lives.

The first thing every liveaboard needs is an address or mail drop. It's impossible to notify everyone every time you move on. Once an address gets written down somewhere, it is a career to get people to stop using it. Aunt Hattie may get huffy if you tell her to send mail to Las Vegas when she knows you're gunkholing the Florida Keys, but trust us. Don't reveal your temporary address to anyone, or the mail will be chasing you forever. The closer the friend or relative, the more annoyed they'll be. Hang tough.

You can have your mail forwarded in several ways. A friend or relative may do it for nothing, or your lawyer, secretary or other professional will give you highly customized service for a fee. The post office can also forward mail (we'll explain that later) for up to a year. A third choice, if you spend all winter in one port and all summer in another, is to notify everyone that you're in Edgartown June through September and Key West October through May. Print that on letterheads, business cards and all correspondence, and it will work about 90% of the time. The rest of the mail can be forwarded. Don't forget to fill out the forms before you leave Edgartown in the Fall and Key West each Spring.

The advantage to having a professional handle your mail is that service goes on full- time and impersonally. Friends and relatives move, go on vacation, fall ill, or get busy. If you're getting sensitive mail, professionals don't look twice at the return address. Friends and relatives, by contrast, may wonder why you're getting bills from a doctor or attorney, or brochures from a hairpiece manufacturer, or loan applications.

However, a trusted friend or relative can do exactly what you want. Knowing the high cost of sending mail to us in other countries, Mom trims everything down to bare bones. She knows that we want to see the boating magazines and college alumni magazine but not the seed catalog. She knows the importance of forwarding bills quickly, so they can be paid in time, but she realizes that Christmas cards can be saved up and sent in one bundle. No amount of money can buy the personal service that you can get from family and friends *who really understand the problem and ways to solve it*. Few do.

When you're languishing in port waiting for a check or a spare part, you may find that a free service is worth exactly what you're paying for it.

The Post Office

The U.S.P.S. will forward your mail free for up to a year but there are problems. One is that forwarding instructions go into a computer that prints out the new (but temporary) address. If the letter doesn't get delivered for some reason and finds its way back to the sender, he or she thinks the forwarding address as a permanent new one and it goes into a database. You've seen the notice "Forwarding Address Requested" on envelopes, usually those used by bill senders. Once, one of our temporary addresses made it back to a credit card company and it took weeks (plus fees and penalties) to unsnarl the mess.

The other disadvantage to dealing with the U.S.P.S. is that everything has to be done in writing. You can't just call up, as you might a friend, to announce a change of plans. By law, they can hold mail for only 10 days. Once we were delayed well beyond our arrival date, so we phoned a small-town post office and explained our plight. They agreed to hold the mail a few days longer. A larger post office probably wouldn't have bent the rules for us. Nor can the U.S.P.S. decide what to weed out. You'll get everything or nothing.

Some post offices are better than others. During one of our snowbird migrations, the northern post office fouled up so badly, we asked friends to forward our southbound mail for six months. However, we could trust our Florida post office to forward our northbound mail for the other six months. In any case, smaller post offices are best. Once in a while, you can drop in face to face and leave a box of candy. You can also remember postal workers with a picture postcard or thank you note occasionally. The other advantage to small-town post offices is that you can choose small, harbor towns where the post office is most likely to be within walking distance of the docks. In large cities, the General Post Office is usually downtown, far from the marina.

Forwarding Services

Commercial forwarding services are more valuable to the liveaboard than ever, thanks to new communications. Many also offer voice mail, message forwarding, fax, and personal messaging reached through a toll-free number. They also offer you a street address, which is essential in those instances where a post office box address isn't accepted.

Best of all, most of them are located in states such as South Dakota, Texas, Florida, Tennessee, Oregon or Nevada, which have tax advantages. Even though you may never set foot in that state, you're a "resident" as far as tax authorities are concerned.

Expect to pay as little as $150 a year for a mailbox plus a monthly fee and the cost of postage. Usually a deposit of, say, $50 is required and you must replenish the account when it runs low. You can also have your own voice mailbox, with an 800 number that any of your friends and family can use to reach you, for about $20 a month. Many services also offer a toll- free number where your friends and family can call to leave a message for you. You pay by the minute to receive the messages.

Companies that provide such services include Mail Call USA, 877-447-2758; Our Mail Travel Service, 800-723-0110; Associated Mail and Business Services, 888-706-0378; Snowbird Mail & Message Service, 800-800-0710; Re-Mail Plus, 800-221-9609, www.dnc.net.mfs; Homebase Oregon, 800-689-8923 or homebase@oregoncoast.com; Keep 'N Kontact, 800-722- 7468; Mail Room Plus, 800-435-9876; Travelers Mail Express, 800-843-7282; Alternative Resources, 800-477-2664 or www.alternativeresources.net; and Travelers Remail Association, 800-666-6710.

When choosing a mail forwarding service look for (1) the widest possible range of features that you want at the best prices. Don't pay for features you don't need, but don't be forced to use several services to get the features you do need; (2) 24-hour access with an alternative way of reaching them if the website is down; (3) human staff rather than only answering machines or a website; (4) a long record of reliability. Start-up companies may not have staying power. You're using the service to get a *permanent* address. (5) A street address in a state with the tax advantages you seek. (6) The most flexible service, allowing mail to be sent as often or as seldom as you choose by as many means as possible. Some services mail only once or twice a month. You may want Priority Mail most of the time, but may require Express Mail or Federal Express in emergencies.

One of the most professional services, Mail Room in

Merritt Island, FL, thinks of everything. First, you receive forms that you sign and have notarized, authorizing them to be your agent for things you may not have thought of such as postage due, certified and registered mail, and COD. They send you a list of tax havens and tax hells and offer you an address in Orlando, San Antonio, or Las Vegas (tax heavens) or New York (tax hell, but the Long Island address looks classy). Their live operators work seven days a week, and they offer 24-hour fax service, lost pet tags, and many more services.

The Florida Mail Room has a nearby State Farm insurance agent in case you need one. You can also register a car, get a driver's license, and vote, all using your Mail Room address. For an additional $19.95 a month plus a per-minute charge, you can get voice mail.

Here are some things we learned about mail forwarding.

1. Have your forwarder label parcels 1 of 1, 2 of 3, or whatever, so you'll know how many total parcels were sent at once. Often we have been handed one bundle of mail but, knowing that Mom had sent more, we asked the postal clerk to keep looking until we had everything. The longer and more arduous the trip from the docks to the post office, the more important it is to get everything that is there for you.

2. Have your mail forwarder use your permanent address as the return address on everything that is forwarded to you. If it goes astray, it will make its way to you eventually, and not back to the original mailer.

3. Creditors, especially credit card providers, often put "Return Address Requested" on envelopes, and the U.S.P.S. dutifully reports each of your temporary addresses. If your mail is forwarded by the post office, the only way to fight this is to write the credit card company, explain the situation, tell them to keep sending mail to your permanent address no matter what, and hope for the best. Still, you'll have hassles. In the computer/voicemail age, machines have no way to deal with non-standard situations.

4. When leaving each port, always leave a forwarding address. If you don't know where you'll make port next, leave your permanent address so mail will go back there. Leaving a forwarding address also reminds the post office, marina or boatyard that you have been there and left. We once returned to a marina four years after our last visit there, and found a few pieces of yellowed mail they had been holding for us all that time.

5. When you order anything by mail, give a street address. Parcel services can't deliver to post office boxes or General Delivery. Nor can they forward. It's also wise to note on the order something like, "Not a permanent address. Do not enter in any databases." This should help in your battle against receiving blizzards of catalogs and junk mail. " If item is back ordered, notify at once. Do not delay shipment." Otherwise, you be waltzed around for weeks, waiting for a back-ordered item.

6. Emphasize to your mail forwarder that certified or registered mail should never be signed for *if it can be re-addressed on the spot.* If it is signed for, it must be re-registered or re- certified before re-mailing. That's expensive.

7. Impress your family with the importance of weighing parcels and using enough postage. If you are staying at a marina and something arrives at the office with postage due, the marina might refuse it and it goes back to the sender. Or, you'll get a postal form instructing you to call for the mail at the post office--and that can be a long and expensive trip. Priority Mail envelopes are one of the best bets. They arrive within the U.S. in two-three days. Stuff the envelope with as much as it will hold, and it travels for one price. This applies only to the Flat Rate Envelope, not the many other cartons and envelopes available for Priority Mail handling.

8. A current Post Office rule, resulting from the fear of letter bombs, requires that any Priority Mail parcels weighing a pound or more must be brought to the post office. When in doubt, ask, or your mail could boomerang right back to you. Like many other businesses, the U.S.P.S. now derails its callers

into an automated phone hell. If you need information on rates and rules, call 800-275-8777 and follow the menu. If you're lucky, the answer to your question will be available somewhere in the cybermaze. We rarely get that lucky. If you need to ask a specific question, dial 0 and prepare to stay on Hold until your feet grow to the floor.

9. Do everything possible to pare down the amount of mail sent to you. Mailing lists are like the Hydra, the mythical creature that grew two new heads for every one that was cut off. When we order anything by mail, we indicate on the order, "Temporary address. Do not place on your mail list." Let magazine subscriptions lapse. Keep sending your name and address to mail preference services, which charge no fee for seeing that your name is taken off mail lists. Notify everyone who mails you that your name is not to be put on any list that they sell or share. Brokers, banks and charities are among the worst offenders here.

10. When you go to a post office to pick up your mail at General Delivery, carry identification. It's often required, and is for your own protection. Even if it isn't requested, however, we write our name on a piece of paper and show it to the clerk. With a name like Groene, pronounced GRAYnee, we can't count on getting the mail just by saying or spelling our name.

Once you leave U.S. shores, the mail picture gets far more complicated and expensive. Mail sent to other countries goes at two and three times the domestic rate. Here's where it really pays off to have a trusted friend or relative who can separate wheat from chaff. In most instances, premium services are fastest and most reliable. The U.S.P.S. offers Global Priority. Federal Express and other parcel services also offer fast, reliable, international service. Make sure you provide a precise address, without abbreviations. Common mis-steps include mail to Dominica going to the Dominican Republic or mail ending up in Austria instead of Australia. Even you may not know the best way to receive mail in a foreign port until after you arrive and get the inside skinny. You may find, for example, that Poste Restante is best or that you're better off getting mail c/o the marina or yacht club.

Here are some tips on getting your mail in foreign ports.

1. In title-aware nations, mail addressed to Captain So-and-so, Yacht Whatisname, may get you more attentive service.

2. Regardless of your grievances against the U.S. Postal Service, you'll find things far worse in most other nations, especially in "manana" lands. The more steamed you get, the better they like it. Relax and enjoy the slower pace.

3. We have been in some foreign ports where the post office was in such chaos, we were invited to find what we could in a huge mountain of unsorted mail! After that, we asked the folks to use some distinctive marker on everything that was sent to us. In a thousand look-alike envelopes, the wink of a day-glo sticker or a bright red envelope will leap out at you. Many times we have spotted our mail across a room after a clerk told us we had none, and sent them to the right spot to find it. Visit a stationery store for ideas on how to make your mail sit up and sing.

4. It's helpful to give your name in writing in U.S. post offices and it's crucial in other countries, especially where English is not spoken. In German, V is pronounced like F; in Spanish, V is pronounced like B. Even in the English-speaking Bahamas, many locals transpose V and W. Write it down in big, block letters.

5. Where possible write ahead to a port and ask that mail be held for you, with emphasis on your name, printed clearly. We once arrived in Grand Bahama, mail-starved after weeks in unpeopled islands, to find that all of our precious mail had just been sent back to the U.S. because a Mr. and Mrs. Greene had just checked out!

6. Advise well-meaning friends and relatives not to send you gifts abroad until after you have some knowledge of how things work there. You may have to pick it up at the customs house, not the post office, and pay duty. It once cost

us two cab fares, duty, and a fee to a shipping agent before we could collect a box of silly Christmas baubles. After you have learned the ropes, you may do better. For instance, a parcel addressed to a Yacht in Transit may not be dutiable. Too, a shirt that has been washed comes in for far less than a new shirt with all the labels intact.

7. If possible, scope out the local situation before giving your mail forwarder a go-ahead. Our mail once ended up on an island where we couldn't go with our 5 ½-foot draft. Another time, we learned that all mail addressed to one marina was piled into a big bin, where everyone could root through it.

8. You may be able to hook up with a local hotel, freight forwarder, or company that has a U.S. address. Your mail can then be flown in with theirs, safe from the local mail pirates.

9. When cruising nearby countries, carry a good supply of U.S. stamps and a small postal scale. Countless times, we have handed stamped mail to States-bound pilots, who were happy to drop it in the first U.S. mailbox they saw. Of course, you can't expect anybody to risk carrying packages for you these days, but small, thin envelopes have a better chance. Incidentally, stamps soon stick together in damp, sea air. Buy peel-off stamps where possible. For other denominations, staple together a "book" made of several pages of waxed paper and place the glue-back stamps between the pages. Never buy a roll of glue-back stamps. It will soon turn into an expensive, solid, papier maché sculpture.

10. When sending mail from foreign post offices, don't forget that you need *domestic* stamps. Your U.S. stamps aren't good outside the U.S. and its territories.

11. International Air Letters are an excellent value. Everything is written on a single sheet, which turns into its own, flyweight envelope. Nothing can be enclosed. We find that this mail somehow travels faster than other air mail.

12. Try to acquaint yourself with overseas postal rates to avoid paying more than necessary. Postal clerks who don't deal often with overseas mail can easily quote the wrong rate.

While cruising in England, we got in the habit of visiting several post offices to get quotes, which varied widely for the same parcel going to the same address. If you're mailing something as heavy as a winch or engine parts, the savings could be substantial.

13. It's always important to wrap items well. In international mail, it's crucial to pad, wrap, and fasten to the max.

14. Before leaving the U.S. order a booklet titled "Know Before You Go" from the Superintendent of Documents, Mail Stop SSOP, Washington, DC 20402-9328. Don't send home anything that is illegal (turtle products, seeds, plants, etc.) or subject to high duties. You can't count on local merchants to know or care that your expensive turtle shell comb or feathered headdress will be confiscated on arrival in the U.S. They're interested only in getting you to buy.

Chapter 12
Doctor at the Dock

Only one thing is worse than having a real gut-wrenching, tooth-grinding, repent-your- sins bellyache, and that is having it far from your family doctor or, worse still, far from any doctor at all. We have taken our share of licks including some cracked ribs in a fall while boarding the boat from the dinghy, a bad head wound suffered in a fall from a ladder while painting the hull when the boat was out of the water, several bad cases of swimmer's ear, and no end of dental disasters. Except for one hospital emergency that occurred while we were in Fort Lauderdale, which has excellent medical facilities, most of our illnesses found us somewhere out in Dire Straits, armed with little more than aspirin and a *Merck Manual*. How can you cope?

Before we moved aboard, we kept having terrifying fantasies about falling from the topmast and fracturing a leg in three places, exotic tropical diseases, appendicitis in some foreign port where doctors speak only Toltec, or having malaria on an island whose only doctor was an American ex-pat who lost his license for habitual drunkenness. Even if you never leave home waters, however, there are special problems for the liveaboard.

In the United States, many doctors no longer accept new patients so, when you are a stranger in town, you may have trouble finding a doctor who will agree to see you. The growing popularity of walk-in clinics is a boon to people like us. Not long ago while running on Flagler Beach in Florida,

Janet came down hard on a board with a nail in it. It went through her deck shoe and deep into her instep. It was a Sunday afternoon, but Gordon got on the CB, asked where we could find the nearest walk-in clinic, and soon we were in capable hands. Between the CB, VHF, asking dockside neighbors, and checking the Yellow Pages, you can find a walk-in clinic in most communities.

Still, most of us put off non-urgent care because of the expense, time, and hassle of going to a new doctor each time. Take heart. We've had very good experiences with helpful, caring people. Usually, other people at the marina are able to suggest a course of action. Once, we called a doctor that another yachtie recommended, only to find that the doctor was on vacation. When we explained that we were strangers in town and needed only a quick visit because of a painful ear problem, the receptionist cheerfully offered to find a doctor for us. "No point in your standing there feeding coins into the phone," she said.

Ways can be found to bring some continuity to your medical and dental care. It became our pattern to haul the boat in Fort Lauderdale and provision there before sailing for the islands each year. It made sense to have our regular checkups there. Our wealthier friends fly from wherever they are to a hometown doctor or to a favorite clinic for their yearly checkups. Any unexpected illnesses have to be dealt with on the go, but at least their records are readily available from one source.

Once you venture into remote places or commit to long periods at sea, things get more complicated. When you leave your home country, complications increase and, if there is a language barrier, can become downright chaotic. One of our doctors even suggested we have our appendix removed as a precaution, rather than risk an attack at sea. (We didn't, but that's how far some people will go.)

Let's go back to basics, well before the time comes to start packing your medicine chest with disposable morphine syringes, scalpels, and pliers for do-it-yourself molar extractions. First comes preventive medicine. Any doctor will tell you to quit smoking, get your weight under control, and exercise. Start with good medical and dental checkups and tie up all the loose ends such as having that suspicious mole removed, your fillings and crowns brought up to date, and so on. If you have been putting off elective surgery, get that out of the way. We continue to meet cruising folk who suffer needlessly with hernias, polyps, piles, bad teeth, and myriad other ills that could have been cured easily. When small problems inevitably become big problems, it is always at the worst possible time and place.

Second, amass as many of your records as possible. You'll be responsible for your own care now more than ever before. Seeing new doctors each time, you must be able to tell them what medications you're taking, what illnesses you had and when, what allergies you have, when you had your last EKG, where to find a copy of your base line mammogram, and so on. Thanks to the Internet, doctors and dentists can exchange information of all kinds including X- rays and other images, but you can't count on every doctor and dentist in your cruising world to be able to access every database.

Carry written prescriptions for eyeglasses and all medications including diabetic syringes, insulin, and other medications that can be purchased over the counter in some areas but require a prescription in others. Leave medications in their original containers too. If Customs accuses you of having illegal drugs, it's helpful to have both the container and a written copy of the prescription. Keep your doctors' and pharmacists' phone numbers handy. Some prescriptions won't be honored out of state.

Talk to your insurance broker about the best coverage for your liveaboard scene. If you're leaving your present plan and have the option of converting from a group to a single policy, don't be too quick to turn it down. The cost will be much higher, but a new physical exam won't be required. Searching for new insurance and waiting out the "preexisting conditions" clause could be even costlier. If you're old enough for Medicare, of course, it's less a problem, but we were in our early 30s when we moved aboard. We opted for a "disaster" policy that would cover us only after we paid the $5,000 deductible.

We recommend continuing your U.S. medical coverage even if you will be cruising abroad. Some yachties let their policies lapse for the sole reason that they plan to sponge off socialized medicine in other countries. In the first place, it's unlikely that you will be accepted as a freeloader. In the second, one look at many of these "free" hospitals will send you scuttling home on the first flight. We had two medical experiences in countries that have government medicine, Canada and the Bahamas. Both experiences were ghastly, medically and financially. Other world cruisers, however, have had superior care in other countries, and for less than they would pay at home.

A surprising amount of free care is available, even in the United States. Watch posters and newspapers for news of free screenings for glaucoma, diabetes, breast cancer, colon cancer, high blood pressure, and the like. Many large hospitals offer free support groups, lectures, and some services. Birth control supplies and information can be found at nonprofit women's clinics. We got our last flu shots at a Wal-mart for $10 a pop.

In addition to health insurance, other insurance options could also be useful to you. We have a policy with Travel Assistance International that provides medical evacuation if one of us is stricken far from home and can't get the care we need locally. Transportation home for the next of kin and the family pet are also covered. Call 800-368-7878. You can also get a list of English-speaking doctors in almost any nation from IAMAT, 417 Center St., Lewiston, NY 14092. If you have a specific problem such as penicillin allergy or diabetes, get a medical alert tag that will alert caregivers even if you are not able to speak for yourself. One source is the Medic Alert Foundation, 2323 Colorado Avenue, Turlock, CA 95382, tel. 800-432-5378.

Access America, 6000 W. Broad Street, Richmond, VA 23230, tel. 800-284-8300 offers a 24-hour hotline staffed by multi-lingual coordinators. They can direct you to the nearest doctor, hospital or legal help in most countries, and can help you get emergency cash or replace documents. When shopping for a travel medical policy, make sure you understand exactly what you are getting for the money. Some provide treatment or evacuation; others provide only information. Many sell short-term policies aimed at people who are going to be abroad for only a week or two. Cost for year-round coverage for the liveaboard would be prohibitive.

Medical Advisory Systems, 800-368-2110 or www.mas1.com offers 24-hour medical advice via radio, satellite, cell phone, land line, or however you can reach them. You pay by the year for access to their service and they keep your medical records on file for instant access. You also pay for any outgoing communications. Some cruising families have been with them for 20 years or more.

When we needed shots for yellow fever, which is not common in the United States, we learned that the vaccine was available only at the free county clinic. We paid for the vaccine but, while they were at it, they threw in smallpox and tetanus shots. When you get immunizations of any kind, get a written record, preferably on the yellow card provided by the World Health Organization. It's one of the most valuable records you can keep on file, if only to keep you from getting needled more than necessary.

Once you have caught up on your insurance and medical, dental, optical, and veterinarian needs (don't forget the family dog and cat), ask your present doctor for help in preparing a medical kit that will be best suited for your liveaboard situation. The more remote your voyaging, the more supplies you will need and the more responsibility you must take for your own care. Medical care in some Third World nations is so bad, it's recommended that you take your own syringes, sterilized instruments, sutures, and even a blood transfusion in case you need it. See the listing for Nitro-Pack and Magellan's in the Appendix.

After moving aboard, we became much more aware of our health-- past, present, and future. After every visit to a doctor or dentist, we make notes in a diary kept just for medical purposes. We also keep a file of medical articles on topics that apply to something we have had or to a country we will visit. If you're online regularly, keep a file on the best web sites too. With each new prescription, we ask for the Patient Information sheet and file them. Not all pharmacies provide one automatically. Ask, so you'll have all the fine print available to any doctor you see in the future. Covered in the PI are dosage, contraindications, side effects, what to do if you miss a dose, and so on.

For years, we also carried our dental x-rays. Today, dentists can send them instantly by computer but, if you can't count on seeing dentists that have this technology, ask for a set of x-rays in hard copy. Once, a dentist was able to make a tricky diagnosis for us by comparing a new picture with an old one.

Fine-tune your own medical kit according to where you will be traveling. It's also good to have a supply of high-voltage pain pills in case you have to tough out a painful injury until you can get to a port. Work out your own list with your doctor and don't forget medicine for diarrhea, minor pain, prescription "uppers" to be used if your life depends on staying awake to bring the boat through a crisis, a good supply of bandages and disinfectants for ordinary cuts and scrapes, and special medications for any children or allergics on board. We prefer an old- fashioned thermometer and sphygmomanometer rather than types that require batteries,

On the assumption that almost everything can be cured by either hot packs or cold packs, we carry chemical ice packs that can be activated as needed (we can't always count on having ice on board). We also carry an ice bag, a hot water bottle, and Aunt Jenny's recipe for mustard plaster. We took our dentist's recommendation for a dental emergency kit containing, among other things, a soft wax to be placed over a broken tooth or crown to cushion the rough edge. He also recommended using Vaseline, rather than commercial dental cement, to temporarily re-seat a crown that comes loose. Often, crowns come off because of decay underneath, and cementing one back would just seal in the decay and create new problems.

Your Medical Library

Most ordinary first aid manuals are no help to the liveaboard who is hours and even days from professional help. One invaluable reference is the *Merck Manual*, which comes out in a new edition each year. The lay reader can't decipher all of it, but it can help you understand and evaluate the care or advice you get from other sources. It's also useful in helping understand symptoms. While self-diagnosis and treatment is rarely a good idea, the book can suggest things to look for, rule out, and communicate to a medical advisor.

The Internet is the ultimate source of medical information of all kinds. If you are told you have galloping epizoodic and want to know all the options available for treatment, you'll find them on the web. The less access you have to firsthand professional care and/or the Internet, the more important it becomes to have a comprehensive, current medical book shelf that includes a first aid book, *Merck Manual* and a book on medications complete with their side effects. Any good book store will give you a good selection.

Earlier, we discussed the importance of keeping a good medical log. When illness and treatment begin, it's crucial to keep up with this log. Enter names of doctors and everyone else who is involved in the treatment, drug names and doses, times, dates, impressions, quotes, and anything else that might be needed later in a dispute over an insurance claim, malpractice, or charges.

In addition to the knowledge in your book shelf, gain personal knowledge by learning the Heimlich maneuver and having your dentist show you how to fix a jaw that locks open when someone yawns too wide. A CPR course takes about 12 hours, but it is well worth the time. There is no substitute for the hands-on experience gained by learning the routines and rhythms on a practice dummy.

Mal de Mer

Seasickness is dreaded by anyone who lives on a boat. We have both been decked by it periodically, usually after being in port for more than a few days. It has nothing to do with training, courage, or intelligence. Even astronauts can suffer motion sickness. It can rear its ugly head any time, although a few lucky souls never feel it at all. It's hard to separate myth from medicine. One of the most persistent stories is that a dab of Vicks Vapo-Rub in the navel will keep you from getting sick. Some people swear by the Acu-Band wrist band that works on the acu-pressure principle and others rely on scopolamine patches.

All the above remedies have the advantage of being non-oral. If you can't keep anything down, seasick pills will come back up before they can do any good. Some cruise ships have shots or suppositories available for victims who can't take anything by mouth. We find, though, that taking a Dramamine at least a half hour before leaving port will usually do the trick. Some people also drink ginger ale, take ginger capsules, drink bouillon, or eat saltines. We've never heard of anyone who was helped by alcohol but, for many, it makes things worse.

Gary Jobson, former America's Cup winner who is a spokesperson for Transderm Scōp, the transdermal scopolamine patch, says, "Getting used to the motion of a boat can take 48 to 72 hours...two to three days is a long time out of commission.... The best remedy for seasickness is prevention." Jobson also suggestions avoiding heavy meals and alcohol before and during sailing. Don't get under-heated or overheated, keep busy, try to stay in the middle of the boat and avoid going below deck. If you keep your eye on the horizon or land, and try to anticipate the boat's motion, you'll fare better.

If you get seasick, says Jobson, lie down or put your feet up. Keep warm, get plenty of fresh air, and have small but frequent sips of liquids. If anyone is sick over the side, put them in a safety harness and lead them to the lee rail. A booklet on preventing motion sickness is available from Transderm Scōp at www.transdermscop.com or 888-726-7724. Jobson can be reached at www.jobsonsailing.com.

Happily Ever After

Living aboard has several medical advantages. We've known young military retirees who planned their cruises around those ports that had the best V.A. hospitals and clinics, and others who sailed to Jacksonville for a visit to the Mayo Clinic or to Miami for heart care. The biggest plus of all is that the liveaboard is fulfilled and happy. You live the way you want to, where you want. You can go where the air is cleaner, the pace slower, crime less threatening, the climate more beneficial. You can live happily, and healthfully, ever after.

Chapter 13
Kids on Board

We'd been invited to cruise for a week out of St. Thomas aboard a sportfisherman with a liveaboard family made up of Mom, Dad, and a 14-year-old lad. He was doing high school by mail in his spare time, worked side by side with his hardworking parents by day, and had also completed a junior college-level course in diesel mechanics. So, he took care of the boat's engines too. He was typical of the dozens of liveaboard kids of all ages that we have met over the years -- poised, resourceful, sea-savvy, reliable, and so bronzed and brawny they make landlubber kids look like sissies.

Although some "boat brats" might turn out rebellious or stupid, we never met a failure. Nor have we heard of a liveaboard child who, returning to public school after mail-order schooling, could not keep up with the class. In every family we meet who cruise as a way of life, there is a quality of cooperation, communication, and pioneer interdependence that one rarely sees ashore. The kids are not necessarily angels, workhorses, or geniuses. They are all, however, smart, self-assured, and special.

We met one couple who had five sons, all living aboard an old, wood sailboat, constantly on the go. Another couple had sailed from Sweden with two of the most beautiful little tow- headed girls. They wore nothing but their faded life jackets. Their little bottoms were brown as bear cubs. We met a Vermont couple, both teachers, who had auctioned everything they owned to buy a boat and go sailing with their

153

girls, ages five and seven. One young couple were sailing the Bahamas with a four-year-old who slept and played in a quarter berth that was her "room". Dad had just finished medical school; this was their time together before he started his practice.

Figure 13-1 Future Products Corporation

Liveaboard kids soon get used to living in their PFDs. This one, from Aqua Force is built right into the swim suit.

Deep in the Out Islands, we met a Long Island couple who got sick of the city and sailed away aboard their 72-foot schooner with seven kids. The baby was still in diapers. We caught up with them five years later, living in a magnificent houseboat they had built themselves. Age 12 was grinding the valves on Dad's jalopy while the girls rowed around the anchorage, taking orders for home-baked goods to be delivered to visiting yachties the next morning. Two younger children were out spear fishing for dinner for the family and for their pet osprey. Dad, an engineer, had a job bulldozing a runway into the island. Mom was doing the wash by hauling water from the cistern and juggling the generator so the refrigerator wouldn't kick in during the spin cycle.

They asked us to stay to dinner, which was cooked by whatever team whose turn it was. After the table was cleared, the kids brought out their projects to show them off. One built model planes. Another had built a kit radio. There was needlework, carving, reading. There wasn't a television set or Nintendo in sight. It was like meeting a maritime Waltons family. Best of all, the practical skills that these kids were enjoying today would serve them for a lifetime.

Fitting Kids Into the Picture

What is needed to live aboard with children? The two most obvious elements are safety, and enough room for them. How much room? Wayne Carpenter, wrote *Voyages with Kristina* about living and cruising aboard a 27-footer with his wife, two daughters *and* mother-in-law! We met one couple with a preschooler, all living aboard a 25-footer, happy as clams. All you need is a bunk for each child, storage space for clothes, toys and hobbies, and a place where school- age children can do their lessons.

Money? Well, one does have to feed, clothe, doctor, and educate children at costs that vary greatly according to family standards, abilities and luck. We met one couple with two children who bought a prepaid college tuition plan before they sailed off into the sunset. Years later, the children would have four years at a state university for a fraction of the current price.

We don't have children ourselves, so it has always been interesting to observe parents' attitudes towards children. A common comment we hear, usually thrown acidly at us by women, is, "You couldn't go off gallivanting like that if you had children." We know full well, of course, that plenty of people go "gallivanting" with their children and have a wonderful life. Also heard often, usually directed at Gordon by a man is, "You don't know how lucky you are, having a wife who is willing to live on a boat."

Figure 13-2

Kids can adapt to living aboard more quickly than adults.

It appears to us that some women use their children as weapons in a war to get what they want for themselves -- a life that does not include a boat. The truth is that kids can adapt to the liveaboard life, with all its joys and hardships, better than adults can. You may have many reasons for not moving aboard, but don't blame those cute kids of yours.

Many shore-side families seem to think of their children as financial burdens who must be coddled and served with every dollar and every hour the family can muster. Most of our liveaboard friends, however, think of their children as their greatest assets. By the time they are eight years old, liveaboard kids are standing watch, quite capably, and taking on other responsibilities that make them feel a real part of the whole. They help with the fishing and foraging, sanding and sailing. They carry their own weight and everyone wins, most of all the kids themselves.

Gary (Cap'n Fatty) Goodlander, author of *Chasing the Horizon* and, *Seadogs, Clowns, and Gypsies,* and many other works, was himself reared on a boat and now his own daughter, who was also reared on a boat, is an adult. If imitation is the sincerest form of flattery, Goodlander paid his parents the highest of compliments by continuing to live aboard.

Safety

When we asked a Halifax friend his secret for peace of mind when living aboard with two preschoolers, he summed up very simply, "Constant supervision." When it comes to safety for children aboard, that says it all. In a sort of buddy system, parents know at all times who is responsible for the children. They are handed over, Navy-style, just as one hands over the helm or the watch. They leave no margin for one of those I-thought-you-were-watching-them tragedies.

Most marine catalogs sell sturdy nylon netting, which can be used to fill in spaces between lifelines where little ones might slip through. Netting can also be used to surround a bunk, turning it into a combination crib and playpen. When our friend Caroline brought her newborn home to the boat, she attached netting securely under the mattress and put hooks overhead. When she needed to get the netting out of the way to tend the baby, she could tuck it under the mattress. When it was needed, it took only seconds to hook it back in place. In addition to creating a safe, cozy nook where children can sleep or play without falling out, make sure nothing can fall down on them if things get topsy-turvy.

Marine stores and catalogs carry PFDs in all sizes from infants on up. Most liveaboard kids wear them as routinely as diapers except when they are safely shut in down below. Keep in mind that PFDs can lose their flotation over the years. Replace them if they get hard, faded, or holed. Another precaution is to use sunscreen on tender, young skin and to protect young eyes from glare by introducing sun glasses and brimmed hats early in life.

Playtime

Toy stores are filled with games and toys that are compact and entertaining for use on board. In addition to all the electronic games and personal entertainment systems, there are all the old favorites including puzzles, musical instruments, coloring books and art supplies, decks of cards, and kits for building models. If a youngster is interested in ham radio, it's a very handy skill to have on board and we have met several young people who got their licenses. Older young people can also do wonders with photography and with supplies for keeping in touch with a pen pal. Chat rooms are great too, but having a pen pal teaches writing skills and gives kids the pleasure of visiting post offices on every island to purchase colorful stamps. This in turn introduces local currency and interaction with native clerks.

Figure 13-3 AB Inflatables

The liveaboard life offers endless fun and learning experiences for children.

We often take relatives or friends' children cruising with us. Among the most popular pastimes are looking at things with binoculars, looking up things in nature identification books, fishing, story books having to do with the sea, making recordings or putting on "radio plays" using a cassette recorder, Silly Putty (but not messy clay), and taking the helm for hour after hour.

No-no's include marbles, which can create a nightmare in a rolling boat, anything with lots of small pieces, any messy paints that require a lot of water cleanup, and magnetic games that can screw up the compass. The perfect example of what not to have on board is jacks. If you've ever stepped on one of these miniature tank traps in your bare feet, you know what we mean.

Home Schooling

When we first became aware of home schooling, it was not yet a political football. Kids in the Australian outback got lessons by mail and radio. Children of missionaries, show business professionals, and oil wildcatters got their lessons by mail because their families moved so often, or because no other schools were available in the remote places where they lived. Until the Internet came along, most home schooling was done by mail.

In years of living aboard, we met only one couple who sent their children to boarding school. The rest used mail order courses, primarily one offered by The Calvert School, 105 Tuscany Rd., Baltimore MD 21210, tel. 410-243-6030, www.calvertschool.org. Still a home school powerhouse, Calvert offers schooling in all levels starting with kindergarten. Best of all, the system is designed to be taught by non-teachers. Instructions are made clear to Mom and Dad, who oversee the course work without having to plan a syllabus, grade tests, or otherwise be professional teachers. Prices start at under $300, ranging to $500-$800 through the 8th grade, with additional courses, such as custom math, available at added cost. Calvert is associated with Johns Hopkins University.

Available from Texas Tech University are accredited curricula for grades K-12. Call 800- MY-COURSE, extension 244. Other sources include Oak Meadows School, Box 740,

Putney, VT 05346, tel. 802-387-2021 and thousands of Internet sites including www.heas.org.uk. On the Internet you'll find (1) accredited schools that offer home schooling, (2) sources that specialize in books and supplies for home schoolers, (3) courses of all kinds through the college level (4) chat rooms where you can discuss home schooling with like-minded souls and (5) government web sites that explain your legal obligations and paperwork in home schooling your children without being charged with truancy.

Using the key words Home school, Home schooling and Home schooler, you'll score hundreds of sites that will help you find the best way to educate your kids on board.

Other families, of course, travel slowly enough that their children attend public schools, especially at the high school level where sports and proms are as important as algebra and physics. It could be as easy as registering for school just as any other resident does, using the street address of the marina where you live (a post office box may not work), or as complicated as many bureaucrats can make things. That's where a support system comes in.

Creating a Support System

Families with children tend to cruise together, keeping in touch by radio or e-mail while at sea, then having happy reunions at the next port. Home schoolers ashore and afloat benefit from networking, putting together group field trips, exchanging books, and sharing resources of all kinds. Maybe Molly's dad can teach all the kids how to make a monkey fist, and Darryl's mom can use a sailor's palm while Beth's mother used to teach physics so everyone needs her help with sticky questions. Kids can get together to learn skills, do chores, and have fun. If anyone plays an instrument, the music lessons and songfests take care of themselves.

In addition, the Internet offers no end of support groups, information, and chat rooms for home schoolers. In many communities, home schooling is politically incorrect to the point where you may have endless hassles. Anti-home school forces portray you as political nuts or religious fanatics. As more and more families opt out of public schools, the more vicious become the attacks against home schoolers.

The liveaboard family faces pressure from several quarters. Even if you don't have school-age children, you're branded a freeloader because you're not paying taxes (never mind that probably half of your marina rent goes to real estate taxes, not to mention what you pay in sales tax, gas tax, ad inf.) If you try to put the kids in local schools, you may have to plead and connive to get them in. However, if you home school and keep them out of local schools, you may have the truant officer on your case.

We were amused to find among liveaboards that about a third wanted to get their kids out of public schools because they are "too liberal". A third think they are "too conservative" and both groups believe -- probably with good reason -- that public schools are too dangerous. The rest just wanted to go cruising, temporarily or permanently. Home schooling is just another of the adjustments that must be made. Thanks to the Internet, it is a more inexpensive, practical, and realistic alternative than ever before.

If you want a structured, mail order Sunday School course with emphasis on evangelical Christianity, try the Concordia Publishing House, 3558 S. Jefferson Ave., St. Louis, MO 63118. If you are looking into boarding schools, see ads in the back of magazines including *Good Housekeeping, Sunset,* and *Southern Living.* Courses at all levels, up to and including college, are also available on Public Broadcasting. Some are national and can be picked up almost anywhere but others are local, and you'll have to stay within range of that broadcast to complete the course.

Chapter 14
The Liveaboard Pet

In March, 2000, a Boat/U.S. magazine reader reported that he was four miles out in Chesapeake Bay when he spotted something bobbing in the water. It was a dog, all alone in the big sea. Fortunately it was wearing a life jacket. The writer scooped it on board, reported to the Coast Guard, and was able to give the dog back to its owners the following day. It was the old I- thought-he-was-with-you story. Mom thought the dog was forward. Daughter thought the dog was aft, with Mom. Meanwhile, the dog had slipped overboard and disappeared while the family sailed on.

If you love pets and have them in your home, you'll continue to want the companionship and help of a pet when you live on a boat. Or, will you? Before you run down to the pet shop, think about the pro and con of having a dog or cat on a boat.

On the plus side, an animal is a faithful friend, entertainment for the whole family, a conversation-starter with strangers, and a very practical accessory. You don't have to go as far as the sailor who named his dog Spare Provisions, but we have known of pets that wake their owners if they sensed an approaching freighter. Big dogs have thwarted break-ins. Even a small dog can warn you of an unwelcome boarder.

Cats are the most effective mousetraps on the market. On board *Cayenne 111,* Ellen and Tony Sanpere even use their cats as weather forecasters. They observed that it always rained within 24 after one cat slept on its back, and a storm always hit within 48 hours after the other cat slept on its back. One night, they noticed both cats sleeping on their backs. Hurricane Lenny, the storm that surprised everyone by arriving in late November well after the end of hurricane season, soon hit them with a Category 4 storm.

There are, of course, problems for you and for the pet. Some marinas won't accept liveaboards with pets. Few topics raise more heat and ire than irresponsible pet owners. No matter how good your pet manners, you're sure to make enemies. If you don't clean up after the pet, you'll get yourself booted out of the marina and probably close the door for future pet owners as well.

You have to walk the dog in all weather, which could mean rowing it ashore or hiking long distances from the dock to find a park where dogs are allowed. However, we once anchored near a boat that had a German Shepherd that had been trained to jump overboard, swim to the island, do its duty, then swim back for the owner to help it back aboard. Somehow, the dog knew not to jump over at other times, when there may not be someone available to hoist it back aboard.

You're living in close quarters, so a pet means more odors, more noise and soil, and less room for you. You need a pet bed, food and water bowls, a litter box for the cat, grooming supplies, and stowage space for large supplies of food and litter. Pets create many extra cleaning problems when they track sand and water aboard, spill food, shed hair, and do gymnastics in the litter box.

Many foreign countries require that pets be quarantined, causing delays and extra expense. It costs money to feed and groom a pet, get medical care, and buy all the extras that are required to keep your pet (and your boat) free of ticks and fleas. The pet can't go everywhere with you, which means leaving it alone on board and hoping it doesn't disturb the neighbors while you're gone. For extended absences, you have to pay for kennel care at $10 a day and up. A teething puppy or a cat with a yen to sharpen its claws can do unspeakable damage to a sail or joinerwork.

Pets have a mind of their own, and we have encountered several liveaboards who had to change their schedule because a beloved dog or cat wandered off. Some of them gave up and left anyway. Others searched for weeks, advertised, offered rewards, and never did find the pet. One scoured a Bahamian island for days, and finally found the family cat, nearly dead from dehydration and starvation, in a deep coral cave. We once rescued a ship's cat that was in terrible condition from licking its salt-crusted fur and having no access to fresh water.

Firsthand, we have been aware of pets that were lost overboard. One was grabbed by a shark before the owners could come about. One was so badly hurt, it had to be destroyed. Some were never seen again. One cat was asleep in a sail that was piled on deck when the sail was suddenly raised, catapulting the cat into the sea. Fortunately, the owner was able to come about and scoop up the cat. One couple woke up one morning to find their cat mewing pitifully and clinging to the outboard rudder. It had fallen overboard during the night and couldn't climb back on board.

One of the worse torments suffered by boating pets occurs because they can't use a marine head and are too well-mannered to go elsewhere. (We have, however, known cats that could use a marine toilet.) During long passages, we have seen dogs suffer in silence because they couldn't use the foredeck, or a newspaper, or whatever they had been trained to use.

Only you can decide whether the service and friendship of a pet will be worth the problems to both the pet and to you. If you do decide to take a pet with you, here are some suggestions.

Health and Well-Being

See a veterinarian about the shots and medications the pet will need for every area you plan to cruise. The shots, and the papers proving the pet has them, are invaluable in foreign ports. You may also need heartworm pills or other preventatives for ills that are not a problem in home port but could be a threat in places you will visit. Some illnesses that afflict pets can be transmitted to their owners.

In our travels, we have met two cats that become miserably seasick. One behaved as seasick humans do. The other had such balance problems, it kept losing its footing and flying around the boat, landing on the most inconvenient portions of its anatomy. Ask your vet about medications for such things, and for a tranquilizer to use in an emergency. A large dog, going berserk at the wrong time, can fill a small boat very quickly.

Find a comfortable, secure nest where the animal can snuggle in, well supported in rough seas. You'll find beanbag-type beds in pet stores and catalogs. Also available are automatic feeding and watering devices, and PFDs in all sizes. It's strongly recommended that you use a pet PFD regularly. If it falls overboard when you're not around, instinct may tell it to stay with the boat and it could exhaust itself trying to get back aboard. If you need to lift a dog aboard, you could hurt it by lifting it by the collar. A PFD with a good lifting handle makes the job easier on you and on the dog.

We were once entertaining guests aboard our boat while anchored in Nassau Harbour, when our guests saw their dog jump or fall overboard from their boat, which was anchored nearby. Ignoring their commands to come to our boat, where it could be lifted aboard, the dog continued to try to stay with its own boat. Paddling against the swift current, it was clear that it would soon be exhausted. Finally, our guest jumped overboard and rescued the pet. This story had a happy ending only because they saw the dog go over the side. Many other stories had more tragic endings.

Keeping Track

Through your vet you can find out about the latest, high-tech tracking systems for finding lost pets. You could go as far as having a tiny transmitter implanted. Also available are tattoos, switchboards, clearing houses, and other services that match up lost pets with their owners. A low-tech solution we use is to place a hollow cylinder on the dog's collar. Inside is our name and current address, which is easily changed each time we move on. The permanent tag can be engraved with your e-mail address, vet's phone number, or other ID, but you'll recover a lost pet far sooner if you have a current address on it at all times.

Special Equipment

Nonskid pet dishes make feeding and watering less messy. Nonskid table mats under the dishes also help keep things in place. We also like to carry a screw-in stake so we can secure the dog in a patch of shade or some other pleasant spot ashore.

Training

It's safer for both you and the pet if obedience is taught. The time could come when your command to fetch or stay or come could save a life. We were on a Midwestern river right after a houseboat blew up because of gasoline fumes. Someone smelled them and yelled Jump! The family jumped, and survived. The dog, who had other plans, did not. Spaying and neutering are also good temper-tamers.

Just as it is with every other facet of your life, the Internet can help with your pet. Buy supplies online, get advice, chat about anything from parrots to pedigreed rabbits, network with other dog lovers, and read an excellent pet magazine at www.pettribune.com.

Good Manners

We once stopped at a marina that banned all pets because one guest, years before, had washed a dog in the shower. The next bather was grossed out at the sight of dog hair in the drain, complained to the management, and the rest is history. While you may see no problem with bathing a pet in the shower, this is second only to dog droppings in turning people against pets. Wash the dog using a bucket, a hose, or inflatable swimming pool, or take it to a groomer. If your dog swims regularly in salt water, it won't need a lot of shampooing, but do give it a freshwater rinse so it doesn't get too much salt by licking itself.

Your pet's meowing or barking may be music to your eats, but to marina owners it could be the swan song for you and all other pet owners. We once spent a month at a marina in the Florida Keys where our neighbors' dog started howling the moment they were out of sight. It didn't stop until the owners' footsteps were heard on the dock. We dreaded their nights out.

It goes without saying that you shouldn't let the dog defecate on the dock but we have seen it happen. The owner immediately hosed it off the dock and thought it was the most natural thing in the world. While most people are more considerate about dog droppings, they are more casual about weewee. We've also seen owners stand and watch unconcerned while a dog lifted a leg on our dock lines. Please be as concerned about liquid waste as solid. Use a poop scoop or plastic bag. There is also a new kitty litter-type substance made for dogs, but it is best for small dogs. For larger male dogs that lift their legs, it's hard to find a container high enough.

Whatever your pet manners, magnify them when you move aboard. Break the rules, and neither thee nor we will be able to find a pet-friendly marina in the future.

Insurance

Could you lose your savings because your dog bites a neighbor or your cat slashes a playful child? Homeowner insurance usually covers such liabilities as this, but your boat insurance probably does not. Talk to a marine insurance agent about the special problems of living aboard.

Adopting a Pet Abroad

Every year, sailors come home with adorable pets they have found abroad, only to find that they can't be admitted into the country. Sometimes it is because the animal or bird is on the endangered list. Other times, it is because the pet is a type that carries certain diseases that can be transmitted to other animals or to humans. Since some exotic pets can cost a great deal, it can be an economic, as well as an emotional shock, to have your beloved wombat or warbler confiscated at your port of entry.

Write ahead to the U.S. Department of Agriculture Plant and Animal Inspection Department, Washington, DC 20229; the U.S. Public Health Service Center for Disease Control, 1600 Clifton Road NW, Atlanta, GA 30333, and the U.S. Fish and Wildlife Service, Department of the Interior, C Street between 18th and 19th, Washington, DC 20240.

Even though you get a clearance from one agency, another agency might nix the entry for another reason, so get information from every possible source. Even so, the import that is approved today may be denied tomorrow because of some new public health scare. And, if you bring in a pet that is worth more than $250, you'll need a customs broker to handle the deal for you. Stick to less expensive, more common pets. Get instructions in advance, and get all the paper work in order.

Chapter 15
Laundry Woes

One of our friends is an ex-liveaboard. Every time she shows a guest her new house ashore, she pauses at the washing machine and showers it with kisses. Only another liveaboard can understand. Among the things we missed most while living aboard were a washer and dryer. If you have enough space and water on board for an automatic washer and dryer, or for one of the compact combination units that wash and dry with one flick of the switch, skip this chapter.

From the first night on board, when you take off your socks, you have a laundry problem. Where to you put the dirty socks tonight and every night from now on? How do you wash them? How do you dry them?

There are many right answers to these questions, depending on where you are and what facilities are available on the shore or in the marina. Our own laundry experiences include the following:

We have taken laundry to dinner parties, at the kind invitation of thoughtful friends. While we enjoy the evening, the laundry spins and cycles. Now that we have a house, it's our habit to invite visiting wanderers to bring their laundry to dinner at our home.

We have lugged laundry bags on our backs to coin laundries as far as five miles away. We have rowed the laundry ashore, dipped water from village wells, and scrubbed as the natives were doing. In the Bahamas, we found water in a cistern in the ruins of an abandoned plantation home on a deserted island.

We have washed in sea water, sulphurous well water, brackish water, and water left over from rinsing dishes. We have dried it on lifelines, on island bushes, on halyards.

It was a rare treat when we were in a marina with a coin laundry. Commercial laundry services are available too, but they have always been out of our price range.

Probably the first shock on that first night aboard is when you realize that everything has been neatly stowed until now. Every locker is full, every drawer assigned. And there you are with discarded socks and no place to put them. Well ahead of time, reserve space for a hamper or laundry bag that will get good air circulation and will be out of the way even as it gets fatter day by day. The longer your passages, the more room you need to stow dirty clothes and linens.

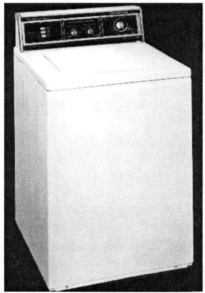

Figure 15-1 General Electric

Down-size appliances and European-style washer-dryer combinations are available in home stores.

Because our boat was so small, even by weekender standards, we couldn't spare an entire locker. We settled for two shopping bag-size poplin bags that were hung in the back of the head. White clothes could go into one; colored clothes in the other. On laundry day, it is easy to throw each in a coin laundry machine, bag and all. Everything goes through a wash and a dry, then folded clothes are carried back to the boat in the clean bags. On long cruises, when laundry sometimes has to wait two or three weeks, soiled clothes and linens can be put into lockers that get emptier as canned goods are used up.

Here are suggestions for making laundry day easier.

First, keep plenty of coins handy. Usually the best hours to use the machines are after the office is closed, when nobody is on hand to make change for you. Treat stains before leaving the boat. It costs far more to buy individual servings of laundry soap and other aids, so buy full-size products and measure them into laundry bags before leaving the boat. If you prefer liquid bleach, carry it to the laundry machines in a small container, preferably one you were going to throw away anyway.

We also recommend adding a product called Dye Magnet to each load. Somehow it soaks up any dyes that leech out of one garment to keep them from staining others. Delicate garments are placed in mesh bags, then washed with a cold water load.

Tuck the fabric softener sheets into your pocket and you're ready to leave the boat. Don't overload coin machines. It's penny wise and pound foolish. Read labels. You'll get a better wash for less money if you don't use more soap and other laundry aids than the manufacturer recommends. Now, after emptying everything into the coin machines except for the fabric softener sheets, you can leave empty handed to do other errands.

As soon as the washers are due to finish, be there! Theft is a problem. Or, an impatient customer who is waiting for a machine (or an angry manager) could take your clothes out and dump them anywhere. I've also had well-meaning friends take them out of the washer and put them in a dryer that was set too hot. After putting them in the dryer and setting the timer, you're free again. Again, be there when the dryers quit! If you fold things when they are still fluffy and warm, they'll look fine without ironing. If they get cold and wrinkles set in, you'll either have to iron everything or spend the week in clothes that look like you slept in them.

Unless you use the same machines often and know you can depend on them, buy detergents that work in cold water. In some remote spots, no hot water is available at all; in others, the electricity or hot water system are always going on the fritz. Don't put a really good garment in a washer you haven't tried before. In one coin laundry, the hoses were hooked up backwards. When a Cold wash was punched in, scalding water came out

Don't crumple soiled clothes into the hamper or laundry bag. If you fold and roll them, as you do when putting them away clean, they'll take up less space and will wrinkle less. Some boating writers scoff at the idea of carrying an iron, but we do carry a small, 110/220-volt iron with a folding handle. Occasionally one wants to fuss over a garment, and several times a year I wash and starch the curtains. For an ironing board, I use a folded towel on a countertop, but pads and small boards are also available if you don't have room for a full-size ironing board.

Hand washing can be done in many ways. If you have room to carry a lidded garbage pail, put the clothes and water in it. Lock on the lid, and let it slosh around underway. We do small items in a bucket. For sheets and other large batches of laundry, we have a child-size swimming pool with inflatable sides. It holds 4-5 gallons of water. You can scrub with a washboard, your hands, or a clean toilet plunger. A ten-minute soak softens dirt. Then scrub, wring, and rinse.

If you will be doing laundry by hand most of the time, use a hand-operated wringer. (Small ones are sold in auto supply stores for use with chamois; hand wringers for home use are also available from Lehman's, listed in the Appendix.)

Clothes will take forever to dry if you can't wring them dry, but we soon found that we were wearing things out very quickly because we each grabbed one end of a large sheet or towel and twisted to the limits of our strength. A hand-operated wringer, by contrast, won't damage fabric so quickly.

Drip-dry clothes haven't been around for decades, but some garments are still best dried on a hanger, starting when they are dripping wet.

Figure 15-2 Gordon Groene

A hotel-style retractable clothes line in the head will come in handy for drying hand laundry or bathing suits.

Salt water can be used to do laundry. Powdered detergents don't make suds, but the liquids do. So does Vel bar soap. Rinse several times with salt water, then do at least one fresh- water rinse with a liquid rinse aid in it. If you can't spare any fresh water, don't wash unless you are truly desperate. Salt stays behind after the clothes dry. The minute the sun goes down, the salt draws moisture back out of the air. The result is damp clothes and sheets, and a clammy smell in your linen locker. If you have no choice but to wash and rinse in sea water, a sprinkling of talcum powder on the sheets and in your underwear will help you feel drier.

There is one other solution to the laundry problem and that is simply to throw things away when you're on long passages. When you're in port, start putting aside any sheets, towels and garments that are nearing the end of the road. Wash, fold, and store them carefully. When you set off again, bring out these items to be used once. Then discard them or consign them to the rag bag. It isn't wasteful. It's just a matter of timing your discards for periods when you don't have access to laundry facilities.

We also save new items, still in their original packaging. to bring out during these periods. New, unwashed fabrics shed soil better and stay fresh longer. Leaving port with two sets of disposable bedding and two sets of new, we change the bed once a week for four-five weeks and still arrive after a month-long passage with only two sets of bedding to launder.

A couple of Grandmother's old tricks work for the cruiser who is on short water rations. One is to carry extra pillow cases, and change only those if you can't manage an entire bed change. Another is to discard the bottom sheet, place the top sheet on the bottom, and add a clean top sheet. For the next change, discard the bottom sheet and add a clean sheet for the top. You might also sprinkle the bottom sheet with talcum. In any case, this system means only one sheet to launder per change, but a bed that still feels fresh and sweet. Grandmother also sewed up muslin "sleeping bags". If you slip into such a bag before getting into the bunk, the sheets or blankets stay clean but the muslin bag is far lighter and easier to wash than a set of sheets. Grandmother's were cotton, but silk bags are available through travel specialty catalogs such as Magellan's (see Appendix.)

To keep clothing and linens fresh, rotate them regularly. In storage in even the driest, airiest boat, things develop atmospheric stains. If you put away some things for special occasions, air them periodically and launder or dry clean them once or twice a year. Never store anything that has been worn or used, no matter how clean it appears. Stains and soil appear out of nowhere. Too, keep salty clothes, towels, bathing suits, and foul weather gear well away from your clean, dry clothes. They'll draw dampness.

Stowing Clothes and Linens

Any homemaker knows that a linen closet should be well aired, but liveaboards know that boating is a wet life. Your boat may have known or sudden leaks, and at some time all of us forget to close a hatch when it rains. So, it's smart to have a few sheets, towels, and tee shirts well sealed in plastic bags for emergencies. Like everything else, these items should be rotated periodically.

As often as possible on dry, bright days, take clothing and linens out for an airing. Use fabric freshener sprays generously, drying well before re-stowing. Put fabric softener sheets in pockets and between stacks of linens, or use sachets.

Chapter 16
Making a Living Aboard

Many liveaboards dress for work every morning, and travel from the marina to the job site just as others travel from their homes or condos. They live at the same dock for years, working for the same company for decades. However, most of the *cruising* liveaboards we have met over the years are not regularly employed. Either they have an independent income, or they retired early -- as early as age 40 with full benefits -- from the military. Early retirement was the buzzword of the 1990s, with golden parachutes and buyouts, and young millionaires who had made fortunes in high-tech stocks. In recent years, however, we are seeing a new breed of home-based entrepreneur who can make a living anywhere in the world via the Internet. The work-at-home mania began with the seven million people who were down-sized or laid off in a ten-year period from the mid 1980s to the mid-1990s. Judith H. McQuown, author of *Inc. Yourself* (Broadway Books) quotes a 1998 survey that found that 64.9% of the jobless moved to a smaller company, 44.2% changed industries to find a job, 18.3% relocated to another region, and the median time for being out of work was 3.48 months. The most exciting thing she found, though, was that 93.3% of the jobless over age 40 started their own business!

Should You Incorporate?

Judith McQuown, author of *Inc. Yourself* says, "Clearly, more than ever, self-employment is the wave of the future and incorporation is the way to obtain enormous tax and fringe benefits and to insulate yourself from liability... I hope that *Inc. Yourself* will help you in your endeavors." If you are working towards an independent life that will allow you to go cruising while still in your peak earning years, this book is a must. Be sure to get the latest edition because tax laws change greatly each year. McQuown also recommends that you work with professionals including an attorney and a tax advisor to make sure you get the utmost benefit from incorporating.

Depending on the state that is your home base, you may be *required* to incorporate. Connecticut, Alabama and Alaska, for example are among those states that require people in all licensed professions -- a charter skipper, for example -- to be incorporated. In other states, only certain professionals must incorporate. However, McQuown points out that anyone is *allowed* to incorporate and she makes a good case for going through the expense and paperwork of doing just that.

The book begins with questions to ask yourself before entering self-employment. If you are now sure that you can support a mobile, liveaboard life with self-employment, answer them honestly. She then explains that you can be a sole proprietor, a partnership (e.g. you and your spouse) or -- and she says this is the most sophisticated and protective approach -- you could become a corporation. McQuown explains that a corporation is a 'legal person', completely separate from the individuals who own and control it. "A corporation has the power to do anything any person may do: carry on business, own property, lend and borrow money, sue and be sued. Most important, it offers its shareholders limited liability. Its stockholders can lose no more than their original investment; they are not liable for the debts of the corporation."

Inc. Yourself makes fascinating reading because it is

filled with case histories and examples of single and married people with and without incorporation. The more you earn, the more you can save, she explains. In a business that brings in $75,000 a year, a married couple will save 23 percent over a non-incorporated couple by taking $25,000 in salary and $50,000 in corporate earnings.

We deduced from reading the book that the best candidates for incorporation are individuals who earn $30,000 to $150,000 a year and who are no older than their fifties. It probably won't pay if you're older than 60 or earn less than $30,000. You must also be an adult, which in most states means age 21 or higher. The younger, the better. She points out that very young entrepreneurs often find it easier to work as a corporation because their clients or customers will take them more seriously.

For some strange reason, laments McQuown, people who work in the computer field can't form a one-person corporation, but she has a loophole. She recommends forming a two- person corporation with a spouse or close relative. That person can perform administrative tasks and receive a small salary. Or, she suggests, you might form a corporation with some other computer wizards. In all other cases, she recommends that you do the numbers before incorporating with your spouse. It may be more advantageous for each of you to incorporate separately.

Inc. Yourself leads you step-by-step through making the decision, filling out the forms, picking a name for your corporation, and setting it up. Throughout the book she points out pitfalls and how to avoid them, especially in regard to the IRS. They keep a close eye on corporations and will put a quick stop to any maneuver undertaken solely for the purpose of avoiding taxes. Most corporations must now use the calendar year as their fiscal year, but she explains that you might get around this by stating a clear, documented business reason why your fiscal year should run from, say, July 1 to June 30. She tells you how to apply for an exemption.

Once you've set up the corporation, go through the

book's checklist to make sure you have done everything right. Then go on to the next section of the book, which covers the why and how of the daunting paper work involved in maintaining a corporation. McQuown makes it look easy. She also explains how other business entities, such as a limited liability company (LLC) or an S corporation, might work for you.

Most of the rest of the book deals with the wonderful new privileges now available to you as a corporation such as "free" insurance, workman's comp, profit sharing and tax-sheltered pensions, investing your corporate surplus, estate planning, and much more. The book's state-by-state requirements for general business and professional corporations are a boon to liveaboards because they can help you decide where to establish a home base for corporation purposes.

All of the time-honored, mobile professions are still open to liveaboards, of course. Rovers can make a living making and mending sails, working on refrigeration systems or diesel engines, selling their arts and crafts, chartering their boats by the day or week, or "temping", e.g. working for a temporary help agency. For as long as we have been on the scene, there have always been cruising folk who sailed the world until their funds ran low, then found any jobs they could until the kitty was filled again. Often we found them working behind the marina counter, waiting tables in a beach front restaurant, turning wrenches at the repair shop, or working as teachers until the school year was over.

Thanks to the growing numbers of people who live full-time in recreation vehicles, a publication has sprung up to serve them and it can also be a gold mine for liveaboards. *Workamper News,* 201 Hiram Road, Heber Springs, AR 72543 can be reached at 501-362-2637, www.workamper.com, or info@workamper.com. A bimonthly, it lists seasonal or temporary jobs for people who live and travel in RVs.

The advantage to the employer is that the worker(s) -- usually both husband and wife work, and many advertised jobs are for couples -- arrive with their own housing. (In your case, that is your boat.) They work for modest wages, and move cheerfully on when the season is over. Most of them are skilled beyond the job level, but they're happy to be under-employed because the object is to keep moving, not get rich. To the worker, the advantage is no-strings employment. You can move on when the season is over with a good reference in your pocket and without appearing to be a job-hopper.

Checking a recent issue, we found that at least 20 percent of the available jobs would be suitable for at least some liveaboards. Many others would work for liveaboards who could commute from a nearby marina. Most of the jobs are in campgrounds, but many of them are on a major river or lake, or on the coast and some of the campgrounds have their own marinas. You can subscribe and simply read the magazine, or run a Situation Wanted ad for $1 a word.

So much for in-place jobs. With the Internet has come no end of additional professions that you can pursue anywhere, even on the most remote atolls. Wireless communications allow you to telecommute to a real job, run your own business, freelance or consult in many fields, and even operate a "store front" in which you buy and sell products entirely online, without ever touching the products yourself.

It's simple, but not so simple that you can tell off the boss this afternoon and have money flowing in over the Internet by the time next week's rent is due. In our book *Get Published, Get Paid* (BookHome Publishing), we recommend that you don't go out on your own until you have (1) enough savings to support you for six months or (2) earn at least 50% of your needs from freelancing. Even if your self-employment is successful immediately, and few of us are that lucky, it takes a couple of months until an even and reliable cash flow kicks in. As they say in show business, don't quit your day job. In addition to an income, you also have to provide for medical and other benefits.

If you need to make a living on the go, carry a professional-looking resume, even if you have to have it prepared by a secretarial service or resume writer. It's also nice to have business cards printed with any address, web site, e-mail or phone you can consider permanent, and perhaps letterheads, invoices, and tools of your trade. If you'll be making a living through the Internet, you'll need a reliable computer system, Internet service provider, and dependable electrical service and a back-up system. We know a heavy-duty software writer who lives on a remote Caribbean island. He has a huge battery bank that kicks in, through inverters, when both the grid and the generator fail.

Consistency and trust have always been important to the wage earner, and that continues to be true in the Internet age. "The computer is down" is no longer an excuse for failing to deliver. The technology is changing with head-spinning speed but we find that the demands and expectations of our buying public (i.e. the publishing world) are increasing just as fast.

A few words of caution about working ashore in other countries. You probably need a work permit and perhaps a visa and other paper work that cost time and money. Even in your home waters, be aware of what licenses apply if you plan to use your boat commercially. Your insurance company needs to know about it too. If a claim is made while your boat was on charter or involved in some other service for hire, and you aren't insured for commercial service, your insurer could fail to pay.

Chartering

Chartering, like writing, sounds like an easy and romantic way to make a living with your boat, but it isn't for everyone. It's akin to running a boarding house or a bed and breakfast inn. You have to welcome strangers into your home, clean up after them, feed them, and keep smiling in hopes they'll leave a tip at the end of the cruise. Some people thrive on chartering. They love the constant company and partying, the grandstanding before an adoring audience, the merriment, the money. Others hate having to put up with the public with all its quirks and faults.

Competition is keen. You're competing with other hungry liveaboards, many of them with bigger or more glamorous boats than yours, and also with bareboat operations and company-owned boats used as tax write-offs.

There are ways to vary the theme, however, and survive in a crowded market. Some yachties sail around the world, collecting passengers who join them for certain legs of the trip. Others call it a "learn to cruise" experience and charge guests outrageous fees for working like galley slaves. Many others do day cruises out of a high-traffic dock, and have the boat all to themselves the rest of the time. You could tie in with a restaurant, a resort, a dive operation. We met one couple with a sport fisherman who took charter guests when they could get them. Between times, they fished their brains out and sold the fish to restaurants.

You might do research charters, eco-charters, sightseeing cruises, business conference cruises, cocktail or sunset cruises, wedding cruises, ad inf. Everything hinges on your being an expert at boating, business, and promotion.

Handywork

If you are one of those people who can fix anything, and have a good set of tools, you can probably make a living on the go just by working for fellow cruisers. The repairs most in demand are radio and other electronics, and air conditioning/refrigeration, both of which require special tools and, in the case, of radios and radar, licenses. Computer hardware repair is also an increasingly popular field ashore and afloat.

Arts and Crafts

The life of an artist, like that of the writer, is not an easy one. The Internet is a great aid to artists like the silk screen painter we met on St. Lucia, selling his work in person and over the Internet, but you can also work flea markets and art shows. If photography is your art, combine your boating skills with the camera to use your own boat as a chase boat and get shots of other boats underway. We know a woman who is a quilt designer. She travels almost full-time with a profession she can practice in person at crafts shows and via the Internet. The more specialized your skill, the easier it is to work the links on the Internet that bring the world to your door.

Teaching, Lectures, and Seminars

If you're a certified teacher, fine. Many school teachers work the ten-month school year and cruise the other two months. We met one couple, both teachers, who found fabulous jobs in the islands, teaching at a private school. You could travel the world, tutoring cruising kids who share your anchorage, or teaching English in non-English speaking countries.

Even if you are not a professional teacher, however, you could also teach your skills of any kind to anyone who is willing to pay. We met an Aussie who ended up in Fort Lauderdale, dead broke after being boarded and robbed off Brazil. Within hours after docking, he had rounded up enough celestial navigation students to start his new nest egg. Another down-and- outer, a woman who emerged from canoeing the Everglades for two years, had nothing left from her marriage but the slides she and her husband took during their sojourn. She went on the lecture circuit and was soon back on her feet. We were impressed at her entrepreneurship. She approached service clubs and other organizations in small cities and offered to put on her slide show for a percentage of the gate. They did all the promotion and ticket sales; she soon had a grub stake to start a new life.

Janet gives seminars on galley cooking and freelance writing. Gordon had a flight instructor ticket that could have been renewed if needed. Many liveaboards are certified scuba instructors, life savers, or board sailing instructors. Resorts worldwide are always looking for nursery school teachers, watersports instructors, and specialists in, say, human resources or spa skills. We gladly pay $60 an hour to our computer teacher/consultant. With computers becoming increasingly essential to the cruising community, you could probably make a living anywhere by teaching others how to get the most out of theirs.

Selling Boats

We've met about a dozen liveaboards whose boat is also their showroom. It's a precarious living but, when you score a sale, it is a very big one. The deals vary, but usually you are able to get the boat at or below cost in exchange for showing it at boat shows. Between shows, you're free to cruise. If you sell any boats between shows, through showing your boat as you go, so much the better. Sometimes you're paid for appearing at the shows and other times you are the sales rep, working on commission. The best manufacturers to approach for this sort of deal are the small, one-off manufacturers who don't have a fleet of demonstrators.

Other liveaboards sell a product aboard their boats. You might use your boat as a showcase for your self-steering system, refrigeration wares, charter service, canvas work, or a line of manufactured products that you "rep." In this case, the manufacturer pays your dockage and show fees, plus a commission.

Treasure Hunting

You don't have to be a Mel Fisher to pick up money on the beach. We've had hours of fun with our simple metal detector. We have never found anything -- the detector is too low-tech-- but some of our liveaboard friends have made valuable finds. If you invest in a detector that can tell the difference between a gold ring and an aluminum pop-top, learn to use it. The happiest hunting grounds are busy beaches on the mornings after holidays and weekends. Regular beachcombers find jewelry, coins, and objects that have little monetary value but for which a reward is offered.

Other good places to hunt are picnic grounds, fields where circuses or other tent shows have just been held, and tidal flats off historic areas. Some of our friends found a 300-year-old brass candlestick in the ooze. Old dumps are good too, not so much because of the metal objects but because you may find old bottles.

Don't use a metal detector in any national or state park, or anywhere protected as an archaeological site. There's a big fine just for *possessing* a metal detector in such areas.

The Sciences

One winter in the Florida Keys, we met young liveaboards who spent their summers off Andros, diving for shells and other specimens for scientific use. As soon as the autumn seas whipped up, they headed for a sheltered harbor in the Keys and lived all winter on the fruits of their summer specimens. Other liveaboards make their vessels available for charter to scientific expeditions.

If you have the academic credentials to collect or scout or study or research something, remember that magic word *grant.* A generous grant could bankroll your liveaboard life while you lay the groundwork for winning the Nobel Prize.

Matters Medical

This brings us into a gray area because, even if you are a licensed doctor or nurse, your credentials won't be good in every country and state where you cruise. Still, there are ways you can make a living while living aboard. A Washington dentist equipped his trawler with complete dental facilities plus accommodations for his children and his wife, a dental technician. Each summer they cruised southeastern Alaska, administering to people in remote logging camps. Although their primary mission was dentistry, they often ended up suturing and providing other first-aid help that nobody else in the area could handle.

If you are a medical professional and don't want to practice, you might sell the medical kits and books that other liveaboards need. Most of us can't find them readily in the marketplace. Serious cruisers need more than drugstore basics.

Boat Remodeling

A few years before we became liveaboards, we read a book by a young couple who made their first million before the age of 30 by remodeling houses. They start with a rundown house that was basically sound, made a small down payment, and moved in. They worked at other jobs by day and spent their evenings and weekends working on the house. They sold that house for a smart profit, invested in another house that had a lot of potential, and remodeled it at a quicker pace because by now they knew the ropes. Soon their profits parlayed to the point where they were able to maintain a nice home for themselves while rehabilitating the wrecks. They worked faster and smarter each time, and were millionaires by the age of 30.

We know the same thing can be done with boats because we have met more than one person or couple who are doing it. It is grueling, dirty work and it's far worse if you have to live aboard amidst the mess while work is going on. It requires a substantial grubstake to buy the boat and everything needed to make it both seaworthy and attractive, and it's a gamble because a downturn in the economy or a change in boating fashion could mean that you're stuck with a boat nobody wants.

Still, some people have exactly the knack, drive, and skills it takes to turn a sound, but shopworn, ship into a showpiece. But wait! That isn't the end of the story. Later, we met a couple who not only fix up boats to sell at a profit, they photograph every step of the way and sell how-to stories to boating magazines. And there is still more. Their reputation grew so greatly among manufacturers who are eager for the exposure, they receive loads of free products to use in their projects. The last we heard, they were no longer renovating old boats but were living on a big yacht they bought with monies earned as how-to writers and television personalities.

If you truly want to live aboard, you don't have to wait until your ship comes in. If you work hard enough, consistently enough, and smart enough, you can find a way to make a living on the go.

Chapter 17
Tools for the Liveaboard

Back in what we call "real life", we had a basement workshop that included a drill press, radial arm saw, a workbench as long as a royal banquet table, and no end of hand tools, power tools, an engine stand, nuts, bolts, greases, goo, paints, solvents, material scraps, and storage space. Sorting and selling it all was like the agony of a peasant farmer who was selling next year's seed corn. We were entering a life where so much would depend on our own tools and resourcefulness, yet we had to give up many of the tools that Gordon had acquired over a lifetime. There was simply no other choice.

Every boating magazine and how-to book publishes lists of tools that the boat owner needs, but instead of giving you a list of things *we* think you need, we put the burden on you, the future liveaboard, to make your own lists. Unlike the weekend boater, you have to live with whatever goes wrong until you can repair it or get it repaired. The weekend boater can throw in the towel, go home for a hot bath, and choose his or her own good time to deal with the broken head. You, on the other hand, not only have to fix it PDQ, you may have to do it using rudimentary tools and perhaps while the boat is standing on her ear. The trouble could be anything from pesky plumbing to a life-threatening hull failure, but you have to deal with it here and now.

There are so many variables, it's hard to know where to begin your list of needed tools. The first is your own abilities.

If you don't know which end of a screwdriver to plug into the wall socket, there is no point in carrying a tool kit worthy of a pit crew chief at Indy. On the other hand, there are sure to be some fittings on your boats that are in unusual sizes. The mechanic or boatwright you hire may not have tools in those sizes, so you have to have them with you even if you don't know how to use them. The same is true of oddball spares that every boat needs. Even if you have to hire someone to install them, it is essential that you have them on board because it's unlikely they can be found elsewhere. The more remote your cruising, the more important it is to have a good supply of tools and spares.

At the other end of the scale is the liveaboard who will cruise far and wide and who can repair anything that can possibly go wrong with the boat and any of its systems. You can make your own list.

Probably most of us are somewhere between the person who can do everything and the all-thumbs person who can do nothing. You may know wood and engines, but need help with radio repairs. Or, you're ace with the varnish brush and spokeshave, but you don't know how to grind a valve. Or you're a great sailmaker and marlinspike sailor, but you don't know anything about refrigeration.

Another variable is the size of your boat. Even if you know how to fix everything, you probably can't have all the tools you want because there isn't room. Heaven knows, a radial arm saw would be handy when you are remodeling, building a self-steering vane, and making custom bookshelves. If you have room for a radial arm saw at all, it has to be a small one. The same goes for a vise, a workshop essential. Even if you have only a small one, it's a basic.

Still another variable is the type and size of your boat. You'll need special tools for steel, fiberglass, wood, or aluminum.

What Do You Need

What is a tool? Basically, it is a device that provides or increases grip, multiplies effort, cuts, or bores. First, sit down with every manual that came with the boat and all its accessories, and list the manufacturer-recommended tools and spares for maintenance and repairs. Most diesel engines, for instance, require a special tool to remove the injectors. Most outboards require a puller of some sort to remove the flywheel without damaging it. Your stuffing box nut will look and last better if you have the right-size wrenches to unlock and adjust it. The old-style, smooth-face monkey wrench is still one of the best tools for the job.

Next, go around the boat yourself, listing the types and sizes of basic tools needed: screwdrivers (slot, Phillips, high-torque); wrenches (metric or inch); circle clip pliers for winches. You may as well get a complete set of combination open end/box wrenches starting with about 1/4 inch and up through at least 3/4 or 1 inch. While you don't want to get carried away with neat rows of complete sets of everything, you'll probably encounter fittings you didn't know you had. You'll also add things later, and someday you may come to the aid of a fellow boater. Buy the set.

Third, and this is the tough one, think through the maintenance and repair jobs you'll be doing regularly: carpentry, plumbing, electrical, rigging, and mechanical. Don't forget tools and spares for things you carry with you, such as the dinghy or PWC, and the tools of your trade, such as your sailmaking sewing machine, or your welder, or computer.

Last, after making lists of the tools you'll need for all the above caretaking and repairs, make sure you also have ammunition for them all: pop rivets, crimp connectors, bits, plenty of extra saw blades, screws, nuts, bolts, nails, staples, sandpaper, printer cartridges, and so on. You'll use lots of moisture dispersant spray such as WD-40 or CRC 6-66, and a good, all- purpose, waterproof grease as well as specialty lubes required by various systems on the boat.

All this list making is tedious, but nobody can do it for you.

How to Buy Tools

The trouble with tools is that they are heavy, awkward and bulky and most of them rust. You've already cut down on the weight and bulk by making lists of things you need rather than gathering up everything from the garage and basement that ever turned a nut or hit a nail. Now shop for:

Quality

Most gripping-type tools will do the job even if they are not the most expensive ones in the store. Cutting tools, on the other hand, have wearing edges that take repeated honing. Cheap saw blades and chisels are a bad buy.

Guarantee

While a guarantee isn't much value if you're on an uninhabited island when the tool breaks, a good guarantee is some measure of a tool's worth. Sears Craftsman tools, for instance, are time-proven classics with a lifetime guarantee. Sears stores throughout the Americas will replace a broken tool for you, no questions asked.

Versatility

Some tools do only one, infrequently needed task and you must have them anyway. Others do more than one job and they become the backbone of the toolbox. A hacksaw, for example, will cut almost anything from wood to metal. A wood saw will cut only wood and plastic. If you can have only one saw, make it a hacksaw. Channel Lock pliers fill the role of pliers, pipe wrench and, in some applications, crescent wrench. A couple of good files can cut almost anything from stainless steel to wood.

Maintainability

Bare iron rusts quickly; forged steel plated with chrome or cadmium will last better. Tools that have working parts, such as a ratchet wrench, should be easily dismantled, using tools you have, for cleaning and greasing.

Independence from Shore Power

Power tools are such indispensable servants that, even though we cruised for months at a time without shore power, we carried a variable speed 3/8-inch drill, an electric saber saw, and an electric soldering iron. Most of our maintenance was done at docks where we had power; only emergency repairs were done elsewhere.

Even better than electric tools are the new rechargeables, which can be recharged on shore power or with the inverter. Early rechargeables were a disappointment but the technology has come into its own and now Skil makes a line of power tools that will run either on shore power or rechargeable batteries.

Still, it's wise to carry manual back-ups. We still have an eggbeater drill, brace and bit, a soldering iron that can be heated on the stove, a butane torch, keyhole saw, and other non-electric tools.

Caring for Tools

The first requisite is to keep salt water away from tools, but sometimes that is a tall order. If they do get salty, especially if they have moving parts, give them a fresh water rinse as soon as possible to float salt out of the joints. Wipe them dry. Use moisture dispersant sprays generously. A spritz each time you put the tools away will help keep them coated. It's also good practice to put cutting tools away sharp, ready to use the next time.

Many costly tools such as a saw, wood plane, or chisels might be put away for months at a time between uses. You might coat them with a rustproofer such as Texaco Compound L, then wrap them individually in paper or plastic to keep the rustproofer goo from smearing all over the toolbox. On the minus side, it's messy. On the plus, side it is self healing. If the coating is cut or weakened in one spot, new goo flows into the void. (Don't use it on *anything* you may *ever* want to paint. Nothing seems to cut it, which is why it is such a superior protective coat.)

If you coat the blade before replacing it in a plane, it's better protected. Tools that can be dismantled, such as the threads of a pipe wrench, can be preserved for long periods with a good rustproofer or undercoating.

Keep tools in the driest place possible. A great variety of toolboxes are available. By shopping in specialty outlets, you'll find just the size and configuration you need. In pickup truck supply places, for example, a tall, narrow toolbox is sold to fit between the wheel well and the cab. Panel truck suppliers sell entire storage systems for people who work out of their trucks. Keep delicate tools in wood boxes for dryness. Plastic and metal toolboxes are poorly insulated and temperature changes can let moisture condense on metal tools.

In addition to tool boxes for protection and storage, you'll need tool carriers for those times when you need to take a set of tools up the mast or into the chain locker or into the dinghy. If you're handy with a sewing machine, use sturdy duck or a light canvas to make a tool "roll" with compartments for a variety of tools. Rolled up and tied, it is a compact bundle. Fabric tool carriers that fit into a bucket are sold in marine stores, or you might zip one up yourself. We also keep one small toolbox at the ready with first-line-of-defense basics, things you grab at the first sign of a breakdown. A belt carrier is good for times when you need both hands free. Most serious sailors also carry a bosun's knife on their belts at all times.

An inexpensive plastic carrier sold for home use is also handy to have in the tool department. Fill it with whatever small tools, spares and cleaners you need for the task and carry it to the job site.

Books and Manuals

The most important tools aboard your boat may not be in the toolbox. They are the how- to manuals written by manufacturers specifically for the equipment on your boat. Take pains to preserve these documents, because sometimes even the best mechanic can't guess at the torque settings for your engine or know that certain types of lubes should never be used on some winches. If your boat is new, keep nagging the manufacturer until you have an entire set. Even the carpeting came with instructions on installation and care and the boat maker does you a disservice if it isn't passed along to you.

It started with computers and now everyone, it seems, is skimping on operator manuals. The books that came with our first computer and our first microwave oven were inches thick, with hard covers. Our newest ones came with nothing more than flimsy booklets that say little (in five languages). Buy manuals, scrounge them, download them. Search used book stores. Beg friends for photocopies. Do whatever it takes to get operator manuals, parts manuals, and/or repair manuals for every machine, every system, every device on your boat.

Tool Suggestions

Figure 17-1 Davis Instruments

A trouble light is always a plus. This utility light has a 15-foot cord, a Fresnel lens, and a bulb rated for 5,000 hours. It draws only .074 amps at 12 volts.

Figure 17-2

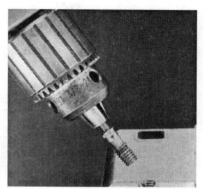

Figure 17-3

Figure 17-4

Figure 17-5

Figure 17-6

Figure 17-7

Figure 17-8

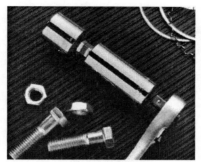
Figure 17-9

Figure 17-10

The above are a collection of Craftsman tools and tool boxes every boater should consider.

Chapter 18
Cleaning and Pests

Housecleaning has changed dramatically in recent years with the appearance of new laminates, chemicals, precautions, products, and surfaces. When you move aboard your boat, you will probably be working with materials you have never cleaned before, such as a fiberglass sink or tub, a marine toilet, textured wall coverings, marine carpeting, and on and on. Moreover, the boat's plumbing wasn't designed to swallow some of the caustic cleaning agents you use at home. The holding tanks have to be handled with kid gloves, and you'll be in deep trouble with EPA if you wash anything overboard.

If you have a salt water plumbing system, which can be very handy in some instances, salt crystals and algae build up in ways you never saw before. Your carpets fill with sand, salt, and fish scales in addition to the usual crumbs and dust bunnies. You wrestle with ways to clean plastic windows and shiny gel coats and decks with rough, nonskid surfaces.

Our rule is to start with the mildest cleaning product possible, then gradually get tougher as needed. Mild soap and water solution, followed by a thorough rinse, is gentlest on the boat's high-priced materials. Sure, you could get things cleaner faster by using a gritty sink cleanser, but just one bath with such a cleanser can ruin a plastic window or coated fabric or fiberglass sink. Even if the abuse isn't immediately apparent, you'll pay a price. As abrasive and acidic cleaners work, they etch surfaces and create tiny voids where mildew and grime can get a better foothold. Each cleaning digs deeper, abrades the surface more and speeds the buildup of dirt.

First, visit a marine store and read labels or talk to a knowledgeable clerk. Marine-grade cleaners cost more, but they have been formulated for marine materials and the marine environment. Many contain oils, protectants, waxes, and/or UV inhibitors that household cleaners do not have, and it's likely they are safer for the environment too. You'll find specialty cleaners for almost every cleaning problem aboard, from galley laminates to the boot stripe. Chances are, there are no better products for the job.

Figure 18-1 Epic

Aboard your boat, you may be cleaning surfaces and substances you never worked with before.

Be especially careful of acrylic ports, hatches and windshields. They're susceptible to scratching. Any grit, even in the clean rag you are using to polish them, can leave scars. If you can't find a special cleaner in a marine store, try the general aviation airport, where cleaners are sold for plastic windows on private planes. Teak is another special cleaning problem. A number of teak cleaning systems are available, most of them using two or three products in sequence to clean and protect this unique wood. If you have a problem with algae buildup in the sump for the shower, look for an algicide sold for air conditioner drains.

Ann Bolderson, who kept her boat sparkling clean for charter guests, told us her secret for crystal-clear shower curtains, which mildew quickly on a boat. When laundering bath towels, add a cup of ammonia to the warm, soapy water (do not add bleach; the reaction between chlorine and ammonia is toxic) and then the shower curtain. Let it go through the wash cycle, and the towels will scrub the plastic shower curtain. Then stop the machine before it goes into the spin cycle. Remove the curtain, and sponge it clean and dry while the towels ride out the rest of the cycle.

Figure 18-2 Black & Decker

You can do just so much with a broom. A vacuum cleaner is a must for getting crumbs out of crevices. If you have room for a full-size vacuum cleaner or a central system, so much the better.

There is a limit to what you can do with a dustpan and broom, so there's no substitute for a vacuum cleaner. Your choices range from a small, handheld rechargeable to household uprights or canister vacuums, to built-in central vacuum systems that are often seen on houseboats. Vacuum often, using a crevice tool to get crumbs out of corners, and you'll have fewer bug problems.

Throw rugs are a safety hazard underway but can be used in port to catch sand and dirt at the entryway and in the galley. Keep a welcome mat on the dock, another on board, and simply shake them in the breeze once or twice a day. For more about choosing, cleaning and maintaining marine materials, see our book *Creating Comfort Afloat* (Bristol Fashion Publications).

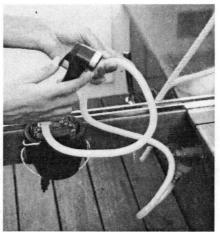

Figure 18-3 Gordon Groene

A sink sprayer can be installed in the head to turn the toilet into a bidet and to aid in cleaning the toilet. Another one in the cockpit helps with cleaning and after-swim rinses.

Bugs

Good screening is essential to keep out flying insects. Don't forget to screen dorade boxes, ventilators, and any other openings where a mosquito or fly could squeeze through. Worse than mosquitoes are sand flies, which we have encountered from the tropics to Nova Scotia. Also called no-see-ums, they are small enough to fly right through regular screens. In desperate cases, smear screens with kerosene or a product called Screen Pruf. It's messy so, rather than treating the screens, you may prefer to find a bug repellent that works for you. Every person's chemistry is different, so it is a trial-and-error thing. We have excellent luck with any of the mosquito repellents against mosquitoes, but sand flies are another matter. Some people find that Avon's Skin So Soft bath oil repels them. If you're in areas where ticks occur, you'll also need a special spray for them. Most mosquito sprays don't work.

In any case, bugs of all sizes and breeds are a part of the boating life. You have all the newest chemicals, but they have millions of years of evolution going for them. Never underestimate their resilience, speed, cunning, and patience.

Prevention

At most docks, rats can jump directly aboard, so make sure every avenue into your boat, including ventilators and dorades, is covered with tough metal screening. Fabric screening will keep out mosquitoes, but larger livestock can gnaw through in seconds. Rat guards are fine for large ships, but are of little use at docks where a rat can simply hop aboard. To keep crawling insects from boarding, encircle dock lines with sticky tape. For those that get aboard anyway, set baits near deck cleats so the bugs will be attracted by them as they climb off dock lines and onto the boat. A cheap and easy bait is a damp sponge dipped in a half-and-half mixture of 20 Mule Team Borax and sugar. Boric acid, which is sold for medical use, is sold in the drug store and is expensive. Laundry borax, by contrast, is less than a dollar a pound.

An old island trick for debugging fresh fruits and vegetables is to dunk them overboard. We have dislodged countless roaches and even some sow-sized spiders this way. However, the idea loses its appeal in filthy, oily harbors. An alternate solution is to dunk all produce in a large pail of fresh water before bringing it aboard.

Some roaches can fly short distances, but most come

aboard with the groceries, the mail, or even in your clothes. A big roach can squeeze into a tiny area -- a corrugation in a cardboard box, for example -- so an eyeball examination is not enough. Unload grocery bags and boxes on the pier and examine each item before putting things below. Never bring corrugated boxes aboard, period.

In most areas, not just in the tropics, it's almost certain that you'll find roaches in provisions, especially in egg cartons and in sacks of potatoes and onions. Their eggs are often found in the glue under labels on canned goods. Foods packaged in unlined bags or boxes (flour, pastas) should be transferred to glass or heavy plastic containers with good lids. Roaches can easily get into most cellophane, plastic, or paper wrapping. Rats can chew through any packaging but metal and glass, including thick plastic storage containers, and it takes them only seconds to gnaw through the plastic, cardboard, and foil packages that hold powdered milk, which they love.

Usually, the tip-off that a roach is at work is a small, oval hole in a bread wrapper or cookie package. You may also see their droppings, which look like poppy seeds, or their eggs, which look like sticky drops of syrup.

Although you can't see any evidence of it, some grains and other dry foods are already infested with eggs, tiny bugs, or larvae when you buy them. Freeze them in a tightly sealed container for 24 hours. Don't open it until it returns completely to room temperature, or moisture will condense on the food. This in turn will attract bugs or, worse still, cause the entire batch to mold or rot. An alternate method is to put a small chunk of dry ice in a container, add the dry food, and let it vent before sealing. Dry ice "melts" into carbon dioxide, which snuffs any bugs.

Work hard to avoid attracting roaches. They can smell decay before you can, often flying long distances in search of a feast. Keep the sink and drain screen clean and dry. Off-load or seal up garbage at night. Pick over produce regularly and discard anything that starts to go bad.

Mechanical Help

There is no substitute for a rat trap, not even a cat that is a good mouser. Most pet cats are no match for dock rats. In ten years of living aboard in the tropics, we had to use our trap only three times, once for a rat that got below at twilight before we had closed up for the night, and twice to catch rats that hopped aboard during the night to scavenge in the cockpit. They couldn't get inside, but we set the traps after hearing them two nights in a row. It's too easy for a rat to steal dry cheese from the trap. Instead, use something sticky such as a dab of peanut butter or a gumdrop.

In ports where flies are a scourge, hang old-fashioned fly paper in the cockpit. Keep fly swatters handy. Spread laundry borax throughout the (dry) bilge, behind drawers, along stringers, and all other behind-the-scenes areas. Use it generously. It's inexpensive, it's a natural product, and it lasts forever unless it's washed away. Yet borax kills any roach that walks through it. We have a big, shaker container filled with 20 Mule Team Borax and it's a ritual for us to sprinkle a little borax in each sink and in the damp shower pan the last thing every night. If a roach is anywhere nearby, it heads for the dampness and tangles with the borax, which kills it. If not -- and we rarely have roach problems -- the borax helps keep the drain sweet and clear.

Treatment

It's one thing to find the occasional roach aboard, and another to have a full-blown infestation of living, breeding roaches. You know you have an infestation if you flick on a light at night and see more than one. Band aid remedies won't work now. You have to kill existing roaches, find and destroy their eggs, and be ready for the appearance of the inevitable hatchlings.

Dismantle the boat as much as possible. Egg clusters

will be found in the most protected areas under drawers and behind sinks. Roaches use wiring and plumbing as an interstate, and they love dark, dank areas under stowed lines and in damp bilges. Scrub and scrape away egg clusters, and clean up roach droppings. Discard packages and labels that appear to harbor eggs. Then treatment with pesticides can begin.

Choose your favorite product(s) and use them according to manufacturer directions. To use them incorrectly will waste money at best. At worst it could endanger your family, your boat, or your waters. When the infestation is finally over, go back to the start of this loop, Prevention, in hopes of heading off the next attack.

Chapter 19
Safety and Security

The U.S. Coast Guard tells you what safety items your boat must have: fire extinguishers, day and night flares, PFDs, and so on depending on the size of your boat and where you sail it. You'll probably want many additional safety devices and back-ups including a solar still, life raft, safety harnesses, Man Overboard equipment, an EPIRB, and so on.

Chapman's *Piloting, Seamanship and Small Boathandling* is still a classic guide to all things maritime, including safety and security. There is a complete list of all the helpful Bristol Fashion Publications' titles in the back of this book.

However, we are talking about *living* aboard, not just safety at sea, and some security concerns are common to us all. The possessions you have on board are not just vacation frills. They may include priceless family heirlooms, your coin collection, the sterling flatware, and all the expensive electronics that go with boating, living, your business, and all your hobbies.

Thanks to the explosion in smart new electronics and sophisticated anti-theft devices in recent years, there are many ways to protect your boat, your possessions, and your loved ones but, before we get into them, a more basic need is to know how to use what you already have. A British cruising sailor we met in Key West told us he had nearly drowned only a few days before, all because his cruising companion didn't know where he kept the extra coils of rope.

Our cruising friend was exploring a shoal in the dinghy, and lost an oar just as the wind freshened. He was out of sight of land and, when the tide changed, he started drifting out to sea. The water was only waist deep, so he began walking the dink back to the boat. Then, as the water got deeper, he began swimming, pushing the dinghy ahead of him. As the skies got darker and the wind stronger, his strength began to wane. He might have sacrificed the dinghy and made a dash for the boat now, but his fatigue was so great that he needed the dinghy for flotation.

Later, his companion said that he could see that the skipper was in trouble, and realized there was a chance of floating a line out to him, but he had no idea where the ropes were kept. Nor did he know how to operate the old-fashioned British-made radio to call for help.

This story has a happy ending because our friend did make it back to the boat, with the dinghy, before his strength was gone. "I can't get over the irony of it all," he shook his head as he told us the story. "All through it, I kept thinking that I'd survived crossing the entire, bloody Atlantic ocean and now I was going to die in shoulder-deep water."

Not every story has a happy ending, even when the boats themselves have every safety device in the world. In one case, radio eavesdroppers listened in horror as a woman screamed for help after her husband fell overboard in the Gulf Stream. She did not know how to bring the boat about. It sailed on, steered by an autopilot, while her husband disappeared in the wake. His body was never found. In other cases, we have listened helplessly for hours while Coast Guard rescuers tried to get a fix on a skipper in trouble who was unable to tell them where he was.

Everyone aboard your boat should know what emergency equipment is available, where it is, and how to use it. Even youngsters can learn how to throw a flotation device overboard, how to signal SOS with a flashlight, how to operate a fire extinguisher, and other lifesaving skills.

Figure 19-1 Fireboy

Most boat fires start from human carelessness.

Extinguishers have to be recharged regularly to satisfy both the Coast Guard and your insurance company. Instead of merely leaving them at a recharge station, take the family with you and ask to set off the charge yourselves. (It's best not to shoot them off anywhere else. The contents may be messy and corrosive. Recharge stations have a place for this.) This gives every family member a real feel for how hard it is to pull the pin or push the lever, how far the charge shoots, and how long the stream lasts.

Inflating the life raft is another matter. It should regularly be inflated, checked, and re- packed by experts, but don't just pull the lanyard to see what will happen. The raft could be damaged if it isn't deployed in the water.

Everyone in the family should know where every piece of emergency gear is stowed and, if they can't use it, know how to get it out and pass it to an adult. As soon as they are old enough, kids should know how to get into their life jackets -- in the dark and in the water as well as under calm circumstances. Older children can have assigned tasks such as helping younger ones. They can learn to use a signal mirror, a solar still, a fishing kit, and the emergency radio(s), and they should know the position of the boat. Everyone should have a flashlight and know where to grab it.

Have regular fire drills and abandon ship drills. Everyone aboard should know how to open hatches from the inside. There are dozens of different hatch designs, most of them difficult and many of them too heavy or tight for children. Guests should know what exits are available. In a panic, most people rush towards the entry door, forgetting about hatches and other exits.

Playing what-if, occasionally ask yourselves what you would tell the fire department, police, or ambulance personnel if you had to describe to them how to find your dock. If your area has a fire boat, can you describe how to find you from the water? If the cell phone and radios are dead, can you find the nearest land line?

We once listened to an interminable exchange between a boat, which had a heart attack victim on board, and EMTs on land. They were trying to determine where the boat could go so the ambulance could meet them. The EMTs had road maps but no charts; the boat had charts but no road maps.

Teach everyone aboard to recognize a collision course. Kids ages eight and older can help serve as lookouts. When another vessel stays at the same relative point on your boat and continues to grow larger while you maintain a constant heading, you are going to meet. At night, when it's difficult to see and translate navigation lights, this technique is very helpful in giving you early warning. It happens very slowly at first, so it takes patience to watch and discern.

Any time fuels are being used aboard your boat (heating, cooking, generator, engine), be alert for signs of carbon monoxide poisoning. Symptoms include headache, ringing in the ears, and perhaps a rosy appearance to the skin. Children are the most susceptible, the first to die. A cluster of houseboats were anchored in a quiet lake under the shadow of protective hills. It was hot, so they were all running generators to keep air conditioners humming. Fumes hung low over the water on that breezeless night. Fortunately, when one child got up in the night with headache and nausea, one of the adults recognized the symptoms of CO poisoning. It's an odorless killer, and its symptoms can easily be dismissed as flu or seasickness. Sometimes in a boat underway, people below can be suffering from CO poisoning while those on deck are unaffected.

In even the tamest and most landlocked boating, it's good to have a Man Overboard drill from time to time. We all think of people getting washed overboard in Hollywood-type storms. The truth is that most accidents happen in calm water. Usually, it is a man who has had too much to drink and is taking a leak over the lee rail. He loses his grip, goes over, and tragedy results if he can't swim, or if the water is extremely cold, or if the current is swift. Keep equipment handy for hauling a person back on board. It takes far more strength than you think, even if the victim can help in the rescue. If the victim is injured and is dead weight, you'll need the dinghy davits.

Practice the occasional "scramble" in which you get away from the dock in seconds. If another boat on the pier catches fire, the best way to save your own life may be to drop the dock lines, start the engine, and save your boat too.

We had two such emergencies. Once, while we were on a borrowed mooring, we were having breakfast when we realized we were adrift in a very crowded harbor. Automatically we hit the engine blower, sniffed for gas fumes, hauled in the frayed mooring line so it would not get into the prop, lit the engine, and steered through the minefield. It has taken us less than two minutes to get underway. Another time, we were ashore enjoying an outdoor movie when a fire broke out in a houseboat on the dock. Our boat was not in danger at that time, but other boats couldn't be moved in time, and were lost. Some liveaboards actually keep axes handy so they can chop dock lines or anchor lines if an immediate escape is called for.

If you live in a marina, take a cue from the Neighborhood Watch program and organize your fellow liveaboards against crime. We were once sitting quietly below when a young man suddenly hopped aboard and stopped cold when he saw the boat was occupied. He came up with a quick story about looking for "Debbie", but it was clear he was here to grab what he could and run. Without making a fuss, we started yelling to all the neighbors in our "helpful" search for "Debbie" while the kid slunk away. He realized that we liveaboards had our own way of looking out for each other. We doubt that he was a problem there again.

Security

Anti-theft devices have come a long way since Joshua Slocum sprinkled carpet tacks on his decks to stop barefoot thieves who boarded him one night. There are countless systems to choose from, starting with household-style alarms that automatically dial the police or fire department and ending with a system customized to your boat and lifestyle.

Start with good locks on the doors, hatches, gas and water caps, outboards, boat trailer, the trailer's spare tire, the hitch, individual electronics, and other special needs. You'll find good locks for special needs in marine stores and catalogs.

In choosing an alarm system, you're basically concerned with reliability, effectiveness in your situation (a loud bell is little help if there is nobody around to hear it), an independent power supply (you can't count on dock power), resistance to dampness and corrosion, and the alarm's ability to differentiate between normal boat motion and boarders. Many of the alarms made for home use rely at least partially on household power and on a land-line telephone. If you live at the same dock year in and year out, such a system could work for you. Installation is usually free or low cost, based on a long-term contract in which you pay by the month.

Do-it-yourself marine burglar alarms have disappeared from the catalogs, but you can have a professional install one for you, or make your own using components from Radio Shack. In addition to alarms that sense intrusion or motion, pressure (such as a footstep on a door mat), and breakage or break-in, have the boat wired for alarms that sense overheat or fire, propane fumes, carbon monoxide, gasoline fumes, smoke, rising temperatures that signal refrigerator or freezer failure, and rising bilge water.

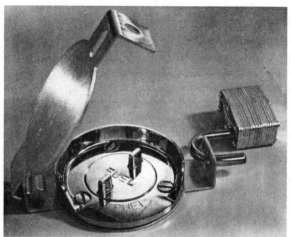

Figure 19-2

This locking fuel fill is a good security and safety measure.

If you are technically savvy, you can wire in alarms that dial your pager, or the police or fire department (beware however, of false alarms because you'll be charged for them). For use underway, alarms are also available to sound a warning if you're on autopilot and veer off course, or if your raw water cooling fails, or if the engine temperature rises. We also like to have a bright light that goes off and on as the bilge pump runs. Underway, when the sound of the pump can't be heard, it helps us monitor whether the pump is running more often or for longer intervals than it should. Lights are, in fact, nice to have in addition to bells and horns that you can't hear with the engine running.

Guns

Whether or not to carry guns aboard your floating home is a topic that is discussed with too much heat and too little light. If you have guns in your home, you'll probably want them in your boat-home. If you are against guns, moving aboard will not make them more attractive to you.

Be aware, though, that having firearms on board will complicate things when you cruise from state to state and be even more trouble in cruising from country to country.

Chapter 20
The Road Back

Every proper story has a beginning, a middle, and an end. For some people, the end of the liveaboard story is tragic: the boat is lost, a spouse dies, a relationship comes to a bitter end, a companion becomes disabled. For many others, the lifestyle merely peters out, retreating into a dreary acceptance of a liveaboard life that has lost its drive, excitement, forward motion, and sense of adventure.

Liveaboards are a strange lot and are the first to admit it. Most of us even admit proudly that we are rebels. Some of the most selfless, hardworking, caring, competent, resourceful, intelligent, and friendly mavericks we have ever met have been part of the liveaboard family.

That family, however, also includes some of the most sour, arrogant, defensive, and bitter people we have ever met. Among the sourest and most bitter are those who cling to the liveaboard image even though they have secretly grown away from the life. They have made some jut-jawed vow to themselves or to each other, and have too much pride or too little gumption to go on to something new.

Fortunately, these two extremes, the sourpusses and the tragedies, are in the minority. Most of us simply come to the end of our liveaboard days and move on to new challenges. Don and Sue Moesly, for example, set themselves a goal of circumnavigating in about five years and then going back to land life and jobs. That is what they did and now, years later, they are preparing to move aboard again.

Others gradually lose interest in living aboard full-time. They move ashore and continue boating as a hobby. One couple gave up living on a boat to buy a farm and raise goats. Another couple built a saltbox house in the beautiful woods of New Hampshire. Others lived aboard only long enough to save up for a down payment on a house, and parlayed that into a fortune in real estate. In our own case, our writing assignments brought so many opportunities to sail everywhere in the world, our own boat became an unnecessary expense and worry.

In his book *Yen for a Yacht* (EPM Publications), Robert Woodbury gave a good description of how some liveaboards come to the end of the road. He describes how "island fever" comes on slowly and subtly. He no longer read menus in island restaurants because he knew them by heart. He made his living by chartering his boat, and he regretted the loss of privacy. He couldn't go anywhere on the island without meeting someone he knew.

For us, some aspects of living aboard began to chafe. One was a bad experience in a boatyard. It reminded us how vulnerable we would always be as long as we had to rely on others to haul our boat/home. We were dependent on others for land transportation and for docks at least part of the time. While our lives were no longer ruled by corporate bosses, we were ruled just as strictly by wind, waves, tides, seasons, and by petty officialdom at home and abroad. When we got together with other liveaboards, the conversation was always about either anchoring, or how smart we all were to get out of Youngstown or Greenwich or Arlington Heights. Like Bob Woodbury, we knew the menu by heart.

It's a common story. One begins to wonder if things would be better with a different boat, or some land for a garden. If only the boat would go faster, or had room for more books. If only we didn't have to move on before hurricane season. If only we had a safe, cheap place to leave the boat so we could fly to Europe for a couple of weeks.

As long as everyone on board gets the same notions at the same time, and a transition can be accomplished with mutual caring and cooperation, leaving the liveaboard life can be as rewarding and exhilarating as moving aboard.

Some ex-liveaboards go back to old careers and the old life. Some take up another form of subsistence life, such as farming, or adventure, such as mountain climbing, or full-time travel, such as RV touring. Many stay on or near the water to work on boats, sell boats, open a waterfront restaurant or beach bar, or start a dive shop. The list of apres-boat success stories is endless.

There is a happy ending to our story too. Just as we didn't throw a hissy fit back in Illinois, walk off the job, and flounce off to sea, we didn't rush out of our boat life either. As our writing income increased, we bought land. A few years later, sure we could afford both the boat and a house, we built a house on our wooded acreage. As our assignments began taking us to more and more places, we saw we could have all the travel and excitement of living aboard without owning a boat. We sold the boat with tears in our eyes, but no regrets.

Living aboard can be indescribably satisfying and enriching. We don't know where we would be now if we hadn't taken that big step, but it's unlikely we would be living self-sufficiently in a small college town, writing books and articles for a living, and cruising anywhere in the world where the notion takes us.

When the time comes for you to leave your liveaboard life, look ahead to the next adventure. You *can* go home again. When and if you do, you will be infinitely richer for having chosen, for whatever length of time, a boat as your home.

Suppliers & Manufacturers

The following list of Suppliers and Manufacturers does not constitute a complete directory of all the fine manufacturers and suppliers available throughout the country. This in no way indicates you should only deal with these companies; as always ask your friends for their recommendations. In most cases you will not be disappointed following their guidance.

AFI: Teak accessories, shelving and organizers. 2655 Napa Valley Corporate Dr., Napa, CA 94558

Alaska Diesel Electric: Engines, 206-789-3880, 4420 14 Ave. N.W., Seattle, WA 98107-0543

Balmar: Alternators and Controls, 902 N.W. Ballard Way, Seattle, WA 98107

Boat/US: Boat Supplies, 800-937-2628, 880 S Pickett St. Alexandria, VA 22304

Camping World, RV Furnishings & Accessories, 800-893-1923, Three Springs Rd., Bowling Green, KY 42102

Caterpillar: Engines, 800-447-4986, 2001 Ruppman Plaza, Peoria, IL 61614

Cummings Marine: Engines, 803-745-1171, 4500 Leeds Ave., Suite 301, Charleston, SC 29405

Datamarine International, Inc.: Electronics Instruments, 508-563-7151, 53 Portside Drive, Pocasset, MA 02559

Davis Instruments: Navigation Instruments and Marine

Accessories, 415-732-9229, 3465 Diablo Ave., Hayward, CA 94545

Daytona Marine Engine Corp.: Engines, 904-676-1140, 1815 N. U. S. 1, Ormond Beach, FL 32174

Defender: Boat Supplies, 800-628-8225, P O Box 820 New Rochelle, NY 10802-0820

Depco Pump Co: Pump supplies and parts, 813-446-1656, 1227 S Linoln Ave., Clearwater, FL 34616

Detroit Diesel: Engines, 313-592-5000, 13400 Outer Drive W., Detroit, MI 48239

Deutz MWM/KHD Canada: Engines, 514-335-3150, 4420 Garand, Ville St. Laurent, Quebec, Canada H4R 2A3

Diesel Engineering & Marine Services: Engine repair and parts, 800-742-1169, P O Box 276, Port Salerno, FL 34992

Dometic: Galley Equipment, 219-294-2511, fax 912-293-9686, P O Box 490, Elkhart, IN 46515

E & B Discount Marine: Boat Supplies, 800-262-8464, P O Box 3138, Edison, NJ 08818-3138

Espar Heater Systems: Cabin Heaters, 416-670-0960, 6435 Kestrel Road, Mississauga, Ontario, Canada L5T 128

Fastening Solutions, Inc.: Heavy-Duty Grips, 800-232-7836, fax 818-997-1371, E-mail fastening@earthlink.net, Web site www.Fasteningsolutions.com, 15230 Burbank Blvd., Suite 106, Van Nuys, CA 91411

Fireboy Halon Systems Division-Convenience Marine Products, Inc.: Fire Suppression Equipment, 616-454-8337, P O Box 152, Grand Rapids, MI 49501

Furuno USA Inc.: Electronics, 415-873-4421, P O Box 2343, South San Fransico, CA 94083

Galley Maid Marine Products, Inc.: Galley, Water Supply and Waste, 407-848-8696, 4348 Westroads Drive, West Palm Beach, FL 33407

General Electric Company, Appliance Park, Louisville, KY 40225

Get Organized: Storage Space Products, 800-803-9400, 600 Cedar Hollow Rd., Paoli, PA 19301, Web site www.getorginc.com

Gougeon Brothers, Inc.: West System Epoxy, 517-684-7286, PO Box 908, Bay City, MI 48707

Hammacher Schlemmer & Company: Unusual Products, 212 W. Superior, Chicago, IL 60610

Heart Interface Corp.: Inverters, Chargers, Monitors, Electrical, 1-800-446-6180, 21440 68th Ave. S., Kent, WA 98032

Home Depot: Tools/Supplies, Located in most cities throughout the country. Look in local phone book.

Hubbell Wiring Device Division, Hubbell Inc.: Electrical products, 203-337-3348, P O Box 3999, Bridgeport, CT 06605

Icom America, Inc.: Electronics, 206-454-8155, 2380 116th Ave. NE, Bellevue, WA 98004

InterCon Marketing Inc., Lighting and Boat Accessories, 1121 Lewis Ave., Sarasota, FL 34237. Web site www.interconmktg.com. E-mail icmmktg@gte.net

Interlux Paints: Varnish, Paint, Coatings, 908-964-2285, 2270 Morris Ave, Union, NJ 07083

Jamestown Distributors: Boat Building/Repairing Supplies, 800-423-0030, 28 Narragansett Ave., P O Box 348, Jamestown, RI 02835

Jenn-Air Company: Cooktop and Ranges, 3035 Shadeland, Indianapolis IN 46226

Lehman's Hardware and Appliances, Box 41, Kidron OH 44636 supplies the Amish, who do not use electricity. It's an excellent source of everything from treadle sewing machines and gas refrigerators to hand-cranked radios and washing machines. www.lehmans.com or e-mail info@lehmans.com. Tel. 330-857-5757 to order a catalog, which costs $4.

Lister-Petter, Ltd: Engines, 913-764-3512, 815 E. 56 Highway, Olathe, KS 66061

Magellan's, 110 W. Sola St., Santa Barbara, CA 93101, 800-962-4943 or www.magellans.com sells travel products including electrical adapters for any system worldwide, security wallets, and a kit containing sterile syringes and sutures.

MAN Marine Engines: Engines, 954-771-9092, 6555 NW 9th Ave., Suite 306, Ft. Lauderdale, FL 33309

Marinco Electrical Products: Electrical products, 415-883-3347, One Digital Drive, Novato, CA 94949

Marine Propulsion: Genset & Transmission Repair, 561-283-6486, 3201 S. E. Railroad Ave., Stuart, FL 34997

Marine Corporation Of America: Engines, 317-738-9408, 980 Hurricane Road, Franklin, IN 46131

Mattresses in custom sizes, shapes and fillings are available from Handcraft Mattress Company, 531 E. Goetz, Santa Ana CA 92707. A sleep system that can be tailored to individual comfort, with dual controls, is available from Americana, 888-565-7211 or www.rvaccessories.com. Custom airbeds are available from 800-508-1008.

MerCruiser: Engines, 405-743-6704, Stillwater, OK 74075

Micrologic: Electronics, 818-998-1216, 20801 Dearborn Street, Chatsworth, CA 91311

New England Ropes, Inc.: All types of line, 508-999-2351, Popes Island, New Bedford, MA 02740

Nitro-Pak Preparedness Center, 475 W. 910 S. Be Prepared Way, Heber, UT 84032, 800-866-4876, www. nitro-pak.com. Fax orders to 888-648-7672. Primarily a supply house for Mormons and others to whom preparedness is a way of life, this company is also a good source of water filters in all types and sizes, multi-fuel lamps, freeze-dried foods and MREs, first aid and dental kits, and other items for the adventurous liveaboard.

Onan: Gensets, 612-574-5000, 1400 73rd Ave. N.E., Minneapolis, MN 55432

Origo, InterCon Marketing Inc.: Stoves and Refrigeration Kits, 1121 Lewis Ave., Sarasota, FL 34237

Paneltronics: Electrical Panels, 305-823-9777, 11960 NW 80th Ct, Hialeah Gardens, FL 33016

PCD, Professional Cutlery Direct, offers cutlery, cookware and chef's tools for the serious galley cook. Everything is professional quality. Request a catalog, PCD, 242 Branford Road, North Branford, CT 06471, 800-859-6994 or www.cutlery.com

Poly-Planar Inc.: Waterproof Marine Speakers, Box 2578, Warminster, PA 18974. Webiste www.polyplanar.com

Powerline: Alternators and Controls, 1-800-443-9394, 4616 Fairlane Ave, Ft Worth, TX 76119

R&R Textiles: Custom Deck Mats, 800-678-5920, 503-786-3678, 5096 Hwy. 76, Chatsworth, GA 30705. Web site www.rrrtextiles.com

Racor Division-Parker Hannifin Corporation: Fuel Filters, 800-344-3286, P O Box 3208, Modesto, CA 95353

Raritan Engineering Company, Inc.: Heads, Treatment Systems, Charging Systems, 609-825-4900

Ray Jefferson Company: Electronics, 215-487-2800, Main & Cotton Sts., Philadelphia, PA 19127

Raytheon Marine Company: Electronics, 603-881-5200, 46 River Road, Hudson, NH 03051

Resolution Mapping: Electronic Charts and Software, 617-860-0430, 35 Hartwell Ave., Lexington, MA 02173

Sea Recovery Corporation: Water Purification, 213-327-4000, P O Box 2560, Gardena, CA 90247

Seagull Water Purification Systems: Water Purification, 203-384-9335, P O Box 271, Trumbull, CT 06611

SeaLand Technology: Marine Heads, 800-321-9886 or 330-496-3211, Fax 330-496-3097, P. O. Box 38, Big Prairie, OH 44611

Star Brite: Coatings/Sealants, 305-587-6280, 4041 S W 47th Ave., Ft. Lauderdale, FL 33314

Statpower Technologies Corp: Chargers, Inverters, 7725 Lougheed Hwy, Burnby, BC, Canada V5A 4V8

Teak Deck Systems: Teak Deck Caulking, 813-377-4100, 6050 Palmer Blvd., Sarasota, FL 34232

The Guest Company, Inc.: Electrical Components, Chargers, Inverters, 203-238-0550, P O Box 2059, Station A, Meriden, CT 06450

Trace Engineering: Chargers, Inverters, 206-435-8826, 5917 195th N.E., Arlington, WA 98223

U-Line Corporation: Ice Maker and Refrigeration, 414-354-3000, fax 414-354-7905, Web site www.u-line.com, E-mail u-line@execpc.com, P O Box 23220, Milwaukee, WI 53223

Unlimited Quality Products: Noise Reduction, 602-462-5235, 800-528-8291, 710 W. Broadway Rd #508, Mesa, AZ 85210

Upholstery Journal/Marine Textiles: Magazine, P O Box 14268, St. Paul, MN 55114

Vanner Weldon Inc.: Inverters & Chargers, 614-771-2718, 4282 Reynolds Dr., Hilliard, OH 43026-1297

Vermont Country Store: Table Cloths, P O Box 3000, Manchester Ctr., VT 05255

Webasto Heater, Inc.: Cabin Heaters, 313-545-8770, 1458 East Lincoln, Madison Hts., MI 48071

West Marine: Boat Supplies, 800-538-0775, P O Box 50050, Watsonville, CA 95077-5050

Westerbeke: Engines, 617-588-7700, Avon Industrial Park, Avon, MA 02322

Woolsey/Z-Spar: Paint, Varnish, Coatings, 800-221-4466, 36 Pine St, Rockaway, NJ 07866

Yanmar Diesel America Corp.: Engines, 708-541-1900, 901 Corporate Drive, Buffalo Grove, IL 60089-4508

Glossary

This glossary has been compiled through a joint effort of the staff of Bristol Fashion Publications and many authors. It is not intended to cover the many thousands of words and terms in the language exclusive to boating. The longer you are around boats and boaters, the more of this language you will learn.

A

Accumulator tank - A tank used to add air pressure to the freshwater system thus reducing water pump run time.

Aft - Near the stern.

Amidships - Midway between the bow and the stern.

Antifouling - Bottom paint used to prevent growth on the boat bottom.

Athwartships - Any line running at a right angle to the fore/aft centerline.

B

Backer plate- Metal plate used to increase the strength of a through bolt application, such as with the installation of a cleat.

Ballast - Weight added to improve a boat's sea handling abilities or to counterbalance an unevenly loaded boat.

Beam - The widest point of the boat.

Bilge - The lowest point inside a boat.

Bilge pump - Underwater water pump used to remove water

from the bilge.

Binnacle - A box or stand used to hold the compass.

Bolt - Any fastener with any head style and machine thread shank.

Boot stripe - Contrasting trim paint of a contrasting color located just above the bottom paint on the hull sides.

Breaker - Replaces a fuse to interrupt power on an electrical circuit when that circuit becomes overloaded or shorted.

Bridge - The steering station of a boat.

Brightwork - Polished metal or varnished wood aboard a boat.

Bristol Fashion - The highest standard of condition any vessel can obtain and the highest state of crew seamanship. The publishing company that brought you this book.

Bulkhead - A wall running across (athwartships) the boat.

Butt connectors - A type of crimp connector used to join two wires end to end in a continuing run of the wire.

C

Canvas - A general term used to describe cloth used for boat coverings. A type of cloth material.

Carlin - A structural beam joining the inboard ends of deck beams that are cut short around a mast or hatch.

Cavitation - Reduced propeller efficiency due to vapor pockets in areas of low pressure on the blades. Turbulence caused by prop rotation that reduces the efficiency of the prop.

Centerboard - A hinged board or plate at the bottom of a sailboat of shallow draft. It reduces leeway under sail.

Chafing gear - Any material used to prevent the abrasion of another material.

Chain - Equally sized inter-looping oblong rings commonly used for anchor rode.

Chain locker - A forward area of the vessel used for chain storage.

Chine - The intersection of the hull side with the hull bottom, usually in a moderate-speed to fast hull. Sailboats and displacement-speed powerboats usually have a round bilge and do not have a chine. Also, the turn of the hull below the waterline on each side of the boat. A sailboat hull, displacement hull and semi-displacement hull have a round chine. Planing hulls all have a hard (sharp corner) chine.

Chock - A metal fitting used in mooring or rigging to control the turn of the lines.

Cleat - A device used to secure a line aboard a vessel or on a dock.

Clevis - A piece of sailboat hardware about two to four inches long that connects a wire rope rigging terminal to one end of a turnbuckle.

Coaming - A barrier around the cockpit of a vessel to prevent water from washing into the cockpit.

Cockpit - Usually refers to the steering area of a sailboat or the fishing area of a sport-fishing boat. The sole of this area is always lower than the deck.

Companionway - An entrance into a boat or a stairway from one level of a boat's interior to another.

Cribbing - Large blocks of wood used to support the boat's hull during it's time on land.

Cutlass Bearing® - A rubber tube that is sized to a propeller shaft and fits inside the propeller shaft strut.

D

Davit - Generally used to describe a lifting device for a dinghy.

Delaminate - A term used to describe two or more layers of any adhered material that have separated from each other because of moisture or air pockets in the laminate.

Device - A term used in conjunction with electrical systems. Generally used to describe lights, switches receptacles, etc.

Dinghy - Small boat used as a tender to the mother ship.

Displacement - The amount of water, in weight, displaced by the boat when floating.

Displacement Hull - A hull that has a wave crest at bow and stern and settles in the wave trough in the middle. A boat supported by its own ability to float while underway.

Dock - Any land based structure used for mooring a boat.

Draft - The distance from the waterline to the keel bottom. The amount of space (water) a boat needs between its waterline and the bottom of the body of water. When a boat's draft is greater than the water depth, you are aground.

Dry rot - This is not a true term as the decay of wood actually occurs in moist conditions.

F

Fairing - The process of smoothing a portion of the boat so it will present a very even and smooth surface after the finish is applied.

Fairing compound - The material used to achieve the fairing process.

Fairlead - A portion of rigging used to turn a line, cable or chain to increase the radius of the turn and thereby reduce friction.

Fall - The portion of a block and tackle system that moves up or down.

Fastening - Generally used to describe a means by which the planking is attached to the boat structure. Also used to describe screws, rivets, bolts, nails, etc. (fastener)

Fiberglass - Cloth-like material made from glass fibers and used with resin and hardener to increase the resin strength.

Filter - Any device used to filter impurities from any liquid or air.

Fin keel - A keel design that often resembles an up-side-down "T" when viewed from fore or aft.

Flame arrestor - A safety device placed on top of a gasoline carburetor to stop the flame flash of a backfiring engine.

Flat head - A screw head style that can be made flush with or recessed into the wood surface.

Float switch - An electrical switch commonly used to automatically control the on-off of a bilge pump. When this device is used, the pump is considered to be an automatic bilge pump.

Flying bridge - A steering station high above the deck level of the boat.

Fore - The front of a boat.

Fore-and-aft - A line running parallel to the keel. The keel runs fore-and-aft.

Forecastle - The area below decks in the forwardmost section. (pronunciation is often fo'c's'le)

Foredeck - The front deck.

Forward - Any position in front of amidships.

Freeboard - The distance on the hull from the waterline to the deck level.

Full keel - A keel design with heavy lead ballast and deep draft. This keel runs from the bow, to the stern at the rudder.

G

Galley - Kitchen.

Gelcoat - A hard, shiny coat over a fiberglass laminate that keeps water from the structural laminate.

Gimbals - A method of supporting anything that must remain level regardless of the boat's attitude.

Grommet - A ring pressed into a piece of cloth through which a line can be run.

Gross tonnage - The total interior space of a boat.

Ground tackle - Refers to the anchor, chain, line and connections as one unit.

H

Hanging locker - A closet with a rod for hanging clothes.

Hatch - An opening with a lid that opens in an upward direction.

Hauling - Removing the boat from the water. The act of pulling on a line or rode is also called hauling.

Hawsehole - A hull opening for mooring lines or anchor rodes.

Hawsepipes - A pipe through the hull, for mooring or anchor rodes.

Head - Toilet. Also refers to the entire area of the bathroom.

Helm - The steering station and steering gear.

Holding tank - Used to hold waste for disposal ashore.

Hose - Any flexible tube capable of carrying a liquid.

Hull - The structure of a vessel not including any component other than the shell.

Hull lines - The drawing of the hull shape in plan, profile and sections (body plan).

I

Inboard - Positioned toward the center of the boat. An engine mounted inside the boat.

K

Keel - A downward protrusion running fore and aft on the center line of any boat's bottom. It is the main structural member.

King plank - The plank on the center line of a wooden laid deck.

Knees - A structural member reinforcing and connecting two other structural members. Also, two or more vertical beams at the bow of a tugboat used to push barges.

L

Launch - To put a boat into the water.

Lazarette - A storage compartment in the stern of a boat.

Lead - The material used for ballast.

Limber holes - Holes in the bilge timbers to allow water to run to the lowest part of the bilge, where it can be pumped out.

LOA - Length Over All. The over all length of a boat.

Locker - A storage area.

Log - A tube or cylinder through which a shaft or rudder stock runs from the inside to the outside. The log will have a packing gland (stuffing box) on the inside of the boat. Speed log is used to measure distance traveled. A book used to a keep record of the events on board a boat.

LWL - Length on the Waterline. The length of a boat at the water line.

M

Manifold - A group of valves connected by piping to tanks to allow filling and removal from one or more tanks.

Marine gear - Boat's transmission.

Mast - An upward pointing timber used as the sail's main support. Also used on power and sailboats to mount flags, antennas and lights.

Mile - A statute mile (land mile) is 5280 feet. A nautical mile (water mile) or knot is 6080.2 feet.

Mizzen mast - The aftermost mast on a sailboat.

N

Nautical mile - A distance of 6080.2 feet

Navigation lights - Lights required to be in operation while underway at night. The lighting pattern varies with the type, size and use of the vessel.

Nut - A threaded six-sided device used in conjunction with a bolt.

Nylon - A material used for lines when some give is desirable. Hard nylon is used for some plumbing and rigging fittings.

O

Oval head - A screw head used when the head can only be partially recessed. The raised (oval) portion of the head will remain above the surface.

Overhangs - The length from the bow or stern ending of the waterline to the forward or aft end of the hull.

P

Painter - A line used to tow or secure a small boat or dinghy.

Pan head - A screw head with a flat surface, used when the head will remain completely above the surface.

Panel - A term used to describe the main electrical distribution point, usually containing the breakers or fuses.

Pier - Same general use as a dock.

Pile - A concrete or wooden post driven or otherwise embedded into the water's bottom.

Piling - A multiple structure of piles.

Pipe - A rigid, thick-walled tube.

Planing hull - A hull design, which under sufficient speed, will rise above it's dead-in-the-water position and seem to ride on the water.

Planking - The covering members of a wooden structure.

Plug - A type of pipe, tubing or hose fitting. Describes any device used to stop water from entering the boat through the hull. A cylindrical piece of wood placed in a screw hole to hide the head of the screw.

Port - A land area for landing a boat. The left side when facing forward.

Propeller (Prop, Wheel, Screw) - Located at the end of the shaft. The prop must have at least two blades and propels the vessel through the water with a screwing motion.

R

Radar - A electronic instrument which can be used to "see" objects as blips on a display screen.

Rail - A non-structural safety member on deck used as a banister to help prevent falling overboard.

Reduction gear - The gear inside the transmission housing that reduces the engine rpm to a propeller shaft Rpm that is optimum for that hull and engine.

Ribs - Another term for frames. The planking is fastened to these structural members.

Rigging - Generally refers to any item placed on the boat after the delivery of the vessel from the manufacturer. Also refers to all the wire rope, line, blocks, falls and other hardware needed for sail control.

Ring terminals - A crimp connector with a ring that can have a screw placed inside the ring for a secure connection.

Rode - Anchor line or chain.

Rope - A term that refers to cordage and this term is only used on land. When any piece of cordage is on board a boat, it is referred to as line or one of it's more designating descriptions.

Round head - A screw or bolt head with a round surface that remains completely above the material being fastened.

Rudder - Located directly behind the prop and used to control the steering.

Rudder stock - Also known as rudder post. A piece of round, solid metal attached to the rudder at one end and the steering quadrant at the other.

S

Samson post - A large piece of material extending from the keel upward through the deck and used to secure lines for mooring or anchoring.

Screw - A threaded fastener. A term for propeller.

Screw thread - A loosely spaced, coarse thread used for wood and sheet metal screws.

Sea cock - A valve used to control the flow of water from the sea to the device it is supplying.

Shackle - A metal link with a pin to close the opening. Commonly used to secure the anchor to the rode.

Shaft - A solid metal cylinder that runs from the marine gear to the prop. The prop is mounted on the end of the shaft.

Shear pin - A small metal pin that inserted through the shaft and propeller on small boats. If the prop hits a hard object, the pin will "shear" without causing severe damage to the shaft.

Sheaves - The rolling wheel in a pulley.

Sheet metal screw - Any fastener that has a fully threaded shank of wood screw threads.

Ship - Any seagoing vessel. To ship an item on a boat means to bring it aboard.

Shock cord - An elastic line used to dampen the shock stress of a load.

Slip - A docking space for a boat. A berth.

Sole - The cabin and cockpit floor.

Spade rudder - A rudder that is not supported at its bottom.

Stability - The ability of a hull to return to level trim after being heeled by the forces of wind or water.

Stanchion - A metal post that holds the lifelines or railing along the deck's edge.

Starboard - The right side when facing forward.

Statute mile - A land mile. 5280 feet.

Stem - The forwardmost structural member of the hull.

Step - The base of the mast where the mast is let into the keel or mounted on the keel in a plate assembly.

Stern - The back.

Strut - A metal supporting device for the shaft.

Stuffing box -The interior end of the log where packing is inserted to prevent water intrusion from the shaft or rudder stock.

Surveyor - A person who inspects the boat for integrity and safety.

Switch - Any device, except breakers, that interrupts the flow of electrical current to a device.

T

Tachometer - A instrument used to count the revolutions of anything turning, usually the engine, marine gear or shaft.

Tack rag - A rag with a sticky surface used to remove dust before applying a finish to any surface.

Tank - Any large container that holds a liquid.

Tapered plug - A wooden dowel tapered to a blunt point and is inserted into a seacock or hole in the hull in an emergency.

Tender - A small boat (dinghy) used to travel between shore and the mother ship. A boat with limited stability is said to be tender.

Terminal lugs - Car-style, battery cable ends.

Through hull (Thru hull) - Any fitting between the sea and the boat that goes "through" the hull material.

Tinned wire - Stranded copper wire with a tin additive to prevent corrosion.

Topsides - Refers to being on deck. The part above the waterline.

Torque (or Torsion) - The rotating force on a shaft. (lb-in)

Transmission - Refers to a marine or reduction gear.

Transom - The flat part of the stern.

Trim - The attitude with which the vessel floats or moves through the water.

Trip line - A small line made fast to the anchor crown. When weighing anchor this line is pulled to back the anchor out and thus release the anchor's hold in the bottom.

Tubing - A thin-walled metal or plastic cylinder, similar to pipe but having thinner walls.

Turn of the bilge - A term used to refer to the corner of the hull where the vertical hull sides meet the horizontal hull bottom.

Turnbuckles - In England, they are called bottle screws. They secure the wire rope rigging to the hull and are used to adjust the tension in the wire rope.

V

Valves - Any device that controls the flow of a liquid.

Vessel - A boat or ship.

VHF radio - The electronic radio used for short-range (10 to 20 mile maximum) communications between shore and vessels and between vessels.

W

Wake - The movement of water as a result of a vessel's movement through the water.

Washer - A flat, round piece of metal with a hole in the center. A washer is used to increase the holding power of a bolt and nut by distributing the stress over a larger area.

Waste pump - Any device used to pump waste.

Waterline - The line created at the intersection of the vessel's hull and the water's surface. A horizontal plane through a hull that defines the shape on the hull lines. The actual waterline or just waterline, is the height that the boat floats. If weight is added to the boat, it floats at a deeper waterline.

Water pump - Any device used to pump water.

Wheel - Another term for prop or the steering wheel.

Whipping - Any method used, except a knot, to prevent a line end from unraveling.

Winch - A device used to pull in or let out line or rode. It is used to decrease the physical exertion needed to do the same task by hand.

Windlass - A type of winch used strictly with anchor rode.

Woodscrew - A fastener with only two-thirds of the shank threaded with a screw thread.

Y

Yacht - A term used to describe a pleasure boat, generally over twenty-five feet. Usually used to impress someone.

Yard - A place where boats are stored and repaired.

Z

Zebra mussel - A small, freshwater mussel that will clog anything in a short period of time.

Books published by
Bristol Fashion Publications
Free catalog, phone 1-800-478-7147

Boat Repair Made Easy — Haul Out
Written By John P. Kaufman

Boat Repair Made Easy — Finishes
Written By John P. Kaufman

Boat Repair Made Easy — Systems
Written By John P. Kaufman

Boat Repair Made Easy — Engines
Written By John P. Kaufman

Standard Ship's Log
Designed By John P. Kaufman

Large Ship's Log
Designed By John P. Kaufman

Custom Ship's Log
Designed By John P. Kaufman

Designing Power & Sail
Written By Arthur Edmunds

Building A Fiberglass Boat
Written By Arthur Edmunds

Buying A Great Boat
Written By Arthur Edmunds

Boater's Book of Nautical Terms
Written By David S. Yetman

Practical Seamanship
Written By David S. Yetman

Captain Jack's Basic Navigation
Written By Jack I. Davis

Creating Comfort Afloat
Written By Janet Groene

Living Aboard
Written By Janet Groene

Racing The Ice To Cape Horn
Written By Frank Guernsey & Cy Zoerner

Marine Weather Forecasting
Written By J. Frank Brumbaugh

Complete Guide To Gasoline Marine Engines
Written By John Fleming

Complete Guide To Outboard Engines
Written By John Fleming

Complete Guide To Diesel Marine Engines
Written By John Fleming

Trouble Shooting Gasoline Marine Engines
Written By John Fleming

Trailer Boats
Written By Alex Zidock

Skipper's Handbook
Written By Robert S. Grossman

White Squall - The Last Voyage Of Albatross
Written By Richard E. Langford

Cruising South
What to Expect Along The ICW
Written By Joan Healy

Electronics Aboard
Written By Stephen Fishman

Five Against The Sea
A True Story of Courage & Survival
Written By Ron Arias

Scuttlebutt – Seafaring Histroy & Lore
Written By John Guest

Cruising The South Pacific
Written By Douglas Austin

Catch of The Day
How To Catch, Clean & Cook It
Written By Carla Johnson

VHF Marine Radio Handbook
Written By Mike Whitehead

Electric Propulsion for Boats
Written By Charles Mathys

About the Authors

While still in their thirties, Gordon and Janet Groene "stopped the world and got off." They'd traveled to Fort Lauderdale to find a boat. Before selling everything, including the power tools, Gordon made new water tanks and a number of accessories for the boat while Janet sewed sheets, slipcovers and duffel bags. With all their remaining possessions loaded into their VW van, they headed south. After stowing everything on board, they sailed for the Bahamas and never looked back.

Janet, who had been writing for newspapers since her junior high school days, began submitting her work to magazines while Gordon took up photography. Janet's first book, *Cooking on the Go,* was followed by *The Galley Book, How to Live Aboard a Boat* and more than a dozen others.

After 10 liveaboard years, when assignments began taking them all over the world, they sold their boat and built a home base in Florida. They continue to cruise worldwide under power, paddle and sail.

Among their honors is the NMMA Directors' Award for boating journalism, two Captain Fred E. Lawton Boating Safety Awards and a Fireboy Safety Afloat Award of Excellence. Janet holds the Distinguished Achievement in RV Journalism Award. Both are members of the American Society of Journalists and Authors and Boating Writers International. Janet is a member of the Society of American Travel Writers and Outdoor Writers Association of America.